WUTHERING HEIGHTS

WUTHERING HEIGHTS

By Jane Thornton

From the novel by Emily Brontë

JOSEF WEINBERGER PLAYS

LONDON

WUTHERING HEIGHTS
First published in 2005
by Josef Weinberger Ltd
12-14 Mortimer Street, London, W1T 3JJ
www.josef-weinberger.com

ISBN 0 85676 280 6

WUTHERING HEIGHTS was first performed by the Hull Truck Theatre Company at the Hull Truck Theatre, Hull on 9th October, 2003 with the following cast:

ACTOR 1
HEATHCLIFF   James Weaver

ACTOR 2
CATHERINE EARNSHAW (CATHY E)
CATHERINE LINTON (CATHY L)   Heather Peace

ACTOR 3
HINDLEY
HARETON
SERVANT   Zach Lee

ACTOR 4
OLD EARNSHAW
JOSEPH
EDGAR LINTON
LINTON   Nick Lane

ACTOR 5
FRANCES
ISABELLA LINTON
NELLY DEAN
VOICE   Louisa Hutchinson

Directed by John Godber

Designed by Richard Foxton

Lighting designed by Graham Kirk

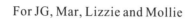
For JG, Mar, Lizzie and Mollie

ACT ONE

*A Victorian theatre stage. A panoramic backdrop of the moors,
leaning towards the abstract. Purples, greens, browns. Rich drapes
over a proscenium. There are five chairs upstage. Actors are on stage
throughout and when not in the scene retire to sit on these chairs
where they sit and observe the action. There are no costume
changes. Centre stage: a large window – frame only – but with a
seat that opens. The window can be moved.*

*ACTOR 3 enters. He puts up a black umbrella as if fighting against the
wind. He creates the noise of wind through his lips and moves
downstage. ACTORS 4, 5 and 1 enter. They too struggle against an
imaginary wind, adding to the sound and putting up black
umbrellas. They stand upstage. ACTOR 2 appears as the ghost of
CATHERINE EARNSHAW. She stands on the seat behind the large
window.*

CATHY E	Let me in! Let me in! I lost my way on the moor. Open the window and let me in! Twenty years it's been. I've been a waif for twenty years!!!!
	(Lights. The ACTORS put down their umbrellas. They shake them simultaneously and take up the story. ACTOR 2 steps down.)
ACTOR 4	In all of England it is hard to believe that there could be a situation so completely removed from the stir of society as the farmhouse . . .
ACTOR 1	. . . at Wuthering Heights . . .
ACTOR 2	. . . as we speak it is evening there . . .
ACTOR 4	. . . and inside the house, dated 1500 . . . and with the inscription . . .
ACTOR 3	Hareton Earnshaw . . .
ACTOR 4	. . . above the principal door . . . are two children . . .
ACTOR 2	Catherine Earnshaw . . . a wild, wick slip of a child with the bonniest eye and sweetest smile . . .

ACTOR 4	. . . and her brother, Hindley . . .
ACTOR 3	. . . a selfish, unlikeable boy . . .
ACTOR 2	. . . they have begged to be allowed to stay up and wait for their father to return from business in Liverpool . . .
ACTOR 5	. . . where he had walked sixty miles there and sixty miles back!
ACTOR 1	Mrs Dean, the housekeeper . . .
ACTOR 5	. . . a worthy woman, who had cared for the children since their mother had died, was waiting with them . . .
ACTOR 4	At eleven o'clock the door latch was raised quietly and in stepped their father. His journey had taken him three days . . .
	(ACTOR 4 *assumes role of* OLD EARNSHAW. ACTORS 2, 3 *and* 5 *assume the roles of* CATHY, HINDLEY *and* NELLY. ACTOR 1 *sits upstage.*)
	Stand back! I'm nearly killed. I'll not have that walk again for three kingdoms!
CATHY E	What have you brought us?
NELLY	We expected you hours ago.
EARNSHAW	I was slowed by the weather. But I have brought you sommat!
HINDLEY	Where is it?
NELLY	Let your father rest.
EARNSHAW	It's in the kitchen.
CATHY E	Can we see?
EARNSHAW	Leave it, he's fast asleep.
CATHY E	Is it a puppy?

NELLY	Not more dogs . . .
EARNSHAW	No!
HINDLEY	A cat?
EARNSHAW	It's a boy . . . a brother. And as dark as he comes from the devil!
NELLY	God save us! Are you mad?
CATHY E	Let me see him!
NELLY	How you can fashion to bring another child into the house when you have your own bairns to feed and fend for, the Lord only knows.
EARNSHAW	He was starving and homeless! Just dumb and laid on the street. No child deserves to live like that, not a soul knew who it belonged to . . . so I thought it best to bring it home!
HINDLEY	I don't want a brother, I want a fiddle!
NELLY	And what shall we call this child?
EARNSHAW	We shall christen him Heathcliff.
	(ACTOR 1 *as* HEATHCLIFF *stands at the window.*)
NELLY	Heathcliff . . .
EARNSHAW	After our son that died. (*As* ACTOR 4.) And it served him, both for Christian and surname.
	(ACTOR 2 *goes to touch* HEATHCLIFF.)
CATHY E	Heathcliff . . .
ACTOR 1	From the first, Heathcliff bred bad feeling in the house! For Earnshaw favoured him and petted him.
ACTOR 3	Which made Hindley jealous.

ACTOR 5   (*sings*) I've known a hundred kind of love –
                 All made the loved one rue;
                 And what is thine, that it should prove,
                 Than other love, more true?

                 (ACTORS 3, 4 *and* 5 *go to sit, then applaud song
                 politely.* ACTOR 4 *rolls a hoop to* CATHY.)

CATHY E   Jump in, Heathcliff! Jump in!

HEATHCLIFF   Let's climb up to the Craggs and chase the rabbits.

CATHY E   We can hide in the bracken; then Hindley won't find
                 us.

HINDLEY   I'll find you wherever you are, you gypsy brat!

                 (HINDLEY *makes a move as if striking* HEATHCLIFF,
                 but doesn't actually touch him. HEATHCLIFF *reacts
                 as if he has been struck but in reality* HINDLEY *is
                 perhaps ten feet away from him. This physical style
                 is used throughout.*)

CATHY E   Leave him, Hindley, you'll tear his clothes then he'll
                 be in trouble with father.

HINDLEY   Father loves him better than either of us. Why don't
                 you play with me any more?

CATHY E   You don't like my games.

HINDLEY   I do.

CATHY E   You don't know how to play them though.

HINDLEY   I'll not let him go.

                 (*He smacks* HEATHCLIFF *again.*)

CATHY E   Stop it!

                 (ACTOR 4 *enters as* MR EARNSHAW. *His health is
                 beginning to decline.*)

EARNSHAW   Leave the boy alone. You've had more than he's
                    ever had.

HINDLEY   Not any more.

EARNSHAW   Don't answer me back, go inside!

                    (ACTOR 3 *goes to sit.*)

                    Cathy, why are you so dirty?

CATHY E   We were rolling down the bank.

EARNSHAW   Not really an occupation for a young lass.

CATHY E   But it's such fun . . .

EARNSHAW   You'll be inside, for your cheek.

CATHY E   But Heathcliff and I are going up to . . .

EARNSHAW   You can stay with Nelly and finish your sewing.

CATHY E   I'll die sat inside . . .

EARNSHAW   What say you, Heathcliff?

HEATHCLIFF   I'll not go without Cathy. It wouldn't be the same.

                    (ACTORS 1 *and* 2 *return to their seats.*)

ACTOR 4   In time, Earnshaw's health began to fail and, more
                    and more, Hindley's scorn of Heathcliff roused him
                    to fury.

ACTOR 3   As a consequence he was sent away to college in
                    the hope that peace would be restored to the house.

                    (*He places a chair DSL for* ACTOR 4 *then returns to
                    sit.*)

ACTOR 5   But it was not to be: from the hour she came
                    downstairs to the hour she went to bed, Cathy was
                    to be in mischief.

(ACTOR 5 *goes to sit.* OLD EARNSHAW *sits. He is not very well.* CATHY *blows bubbles which she takes from the window seat.*)

CATHY E   Catch them, Heathcliff, before they're taken on the wind!

HEATHCLIFF   I can't!

(CATHY *blows again. They go all over* OLD EARNSHAW. *He coughs.* CATHY *and* HEATHCLIFF *are laughing.*)

EARNSHAW   Why canst thou not always be a good lass?

CATHY E   Why can't you always be good, father?

EARNSHAW   I'll have less of your cheek and all.

(*He coughs again.* CATHY *kisses his hand and kneels beside him. She passes the bubbles to* HEATHCLIFF.)

CATHY E   Let me sing you to sleep then.

             (*sings*) The sun has set and the long grass now
             Waves drearily in the evening wind
             And the wild bird has flown from that old grey stone
             In some warm nook a couch to find.

             (*As* CATHY *sings,* EARNSHAW'S *fingers drop from hers and his head sinks on his chest.* ACTOR 5 *approaches as* NELLY.)

NELLY   Mr Earnshaw, don't sleep here, go to your bed!

CATHY E   Father . . .

NELLY   Hush, child.

CATHY E   Father . . .

NELLY   Go upstairs, children.

CATHY E	Let me kiss him goodnight.
NELLY	No.

(ACTOR 4 *rises and takes his chair.* ACTOR 3 *puts up an umbrella. This motif is used throughout whenever a death occurs.*)

CATHY E	Father . . . father! He's dead, Heathcliff! He's dead!

(*A cry from* HEATHCLIFF *and* CATHY. *All* ACTORS *gather in front of the window frame and form a tableau as if at a funeral. They make the noise of the wind.* ACTOR 3 *passes umbrella to* ACTOR 1 *who shakes it and goes to sit.*)

ACTOR 3	When Hindley came home for the funeral he had altered considerably; grown sparer, dressed differently, and to everyone's amazement he brought with him a wife.
ACTOR 5	She was thin, but young and fresh-complexioned. Her eyes sparkled as bright as diamonds but she had a troublesome cough.

(ACTOR 5 *becomes* FRANCES. *She starts coughing.* ACTORS 1 *and* 4 *cough and move back to sit.*)

HINDLEY	Frances is to be the new mistress of the house.
FRANCES	It's so beautiful here.
CATHY E	Not when the rain's driving through the trees . . .
FRANCES	I've been so longing to meet you.
CATHY E	. . . and the wind rattles around the house.
FRANCES	Tell me, are the mourners gone yet? I can't bear to see people in black. It makes me so afraid.

(*She coughs again.*)

HINDLEY	From now on the servants must quarter themselves in the back kitchen and leave the house for us. We'll carpet and paper a small spare room for a parlour . . .
FRANCES	But there is no need, I love it as it is.
CATHY E	What are you afraid of?
FRANCES	You know I'm going to so love having a sister but that boy . . . Heathcliff . . .
HINDLEY	He'll not trouble you, from now on he will stay with the servants and labour outdoors like the others . . .
CATHY E	That's not what father wanted.
HINDLEY	Father's not here. Things are going to change.
CATHY E	Then I'll stay outside with him.
FRANCES	Oh, Cathy.
CATHY E	I will.
HINDLEY	Then you shall go without dinner or supper.
FRANCES	She doesn't mean it. Do you, sister?
CATHY E	Yes, I do!
	(*Lights. Music.* ACTORS 3 *and* 4 *go to sit.* CATHY *and* HEATHCLIFF *sit under window on the floor.*)
CATHY E	I think she expects me to sit with her by the fireside.
HEATHCLIFF	He only came back for revenge.
CATHY E	I don't want to be like her. I want me and you to live wild on the moors and grow up as rude as savages – promise me we will.
HEATHCLIFF	I promise. And I promise I'll get Hindley back.

CATHY E Let's cross the moors now and go to the Grange.

(*They stand.*)

HEATHCLIFF We'll miss supper.

CATHY E I'm to miss it anyway! Come on, I'll race you. We'll see how the Lintons in their big house and fancy clothes pass their Sunday evenings.

HEATHCLIFF Who cares?

CATHY E I do.

(*They make a move forward.* ACTORS 4 *and* 5 *assume the roles of* EDGAR *and* ISABELLA LINTON, *forming a tableau upstage, and within the frame of the window.*)

ACTOR 1 They ran from the top of the heights to the park without stopping, then crept through a broken hedge, groped a path and planted themselves on a flower pot under the drawing room window.

(CATHY *and* HEATHCLIFF *turn and throw themselves below the window.*)

ACTOR 4 The Linton children: Edgar, a fair-haired and graceful boy . . .

ACTOR 5 . . . and his younger sister Isabella: strong-willed and temperamental . . .

ACTOR 4 . . . had the room to themselves and were arguing over a toy.

(EDGAR LINTON *sits on window seat facing upstage watching his sister.* ISABELLA *mimes holding a string puppet.*)

ISABELLA I had it first, it was my idea to do a play.

EDGAR But it's my puppet.

ISABELLA   Sit down, you're supposed to be the audience.

EDGAR   You cannot perform a play with one puppet alone.

ISABELLA   You don't know the story, Edgar.

EDGAR   Well I won't listen, so there!

               (ACTORS 4 *and* 5 *freeze.* CATHY *and* HEATHCLIFF *peer in through the windows. They laugh at* EDGAR *and* ISABELLA.)

HEATHCLIFF   Is that their pleasure, to quarrel?

CATHY E   When would we yell and sob and roll on the ground?

HEATHCLIFF   I'd not exchange for a thousand lives my condition for Edgar Linton's. Not if I had the privilege of painting the house-front with Hindley's blood. Look at him!

               (*They laugh out loud and are heard by the Lintons.*)

ISABELLA   Edgar, get up! Get up! I think someone's outside. I heard something by the window. Call the servants!

EDGAR   Someone come quickly!

HEATHCLIFF   They've let the bulldog out!

CATHY E   Go without me, you'll be quicker.

HEATHCLIFF   I'll carry you.

CATHY E   Go without me.

HEATHCLIFF   No . . .

               (ACTOR 4 *makes sound of a dog barking.* ACTOR 3 *comes downstage quickly as if holding the bulldog on a leash.* CATHY *screams and falls back onto* HEATHCLIFF *as if the dog has bitten her foot.* HEATHCLIFF *holds her.*)

ACTOR 3	(*as* SERVANT) Skulker has caught a girl, sir, and there's a lad here. Very like robbers were putting them through the window to open the doors for the gang after we were asleep.
	(EDGAR *and* ISABELLA *peer through the window.*)
EDGAR	Isn't that Miss Earnshaw?
ISABELLA	Miss Earnshaw wouldn't be scouring the country with a gypsy.
ACTOR 3	The child is in mourning – maybe it is.
EDGAR	And she may be lamed for life. Is your name Catherine?
CATHY E	Yes!
ISABELLA	How careless then your brother is for letting you run wild like this.
EDGAR	Who is the boy?
CATHY E	Heathcliff.
ISABELLA	What a wicked boy, quite unfit for a decent house. Take him away!
HEATHCLIFF	I'll not go without Cathy.
CATHY E	They'll send me home later in the carriage.
ACTOR 3	Begone with you!
HEATHCLIFF	Cathy!
CATHY E	Tell Nelly where I am.
	(HEATHCLIFF *scowls and goes to sit.*)
EDGAR	Bring Miss Cathy some cakes.
ISABELLA	And a basin of warm water to wash her feet.

ACTOR 3 Sir . . .

EDGAR We shall stay by the warm fire and wait for Papa and Mama to come back from Evensong. They'll know what to do.

ISABELLA Yes, and I shall go and get a comb and then I'll do your beautiful hair.

CATHY E Will the cakes be long?

EDGAR (*laughing*) Why? Are you hungry?

CATHY E Very!

  (*More laughter.* ACTOR 5 *sings the first four lines of "God Rest Ye Merry Gentlemen" as* ACTORS 3 *and* 4 *return to their seats. At the end of the verse the others applaud her, then she, too, returns to her seat.* ACTOR 2 *has now stood.*)

ACTOR 2 Cathy stayed at Thrushcross Grange for five weeks till Christmas. By that time her ankle was thoroughly cured, and her manners much improved.

ACTOR 1 Instead of a wild, hatless little savage returning to the Heights, there alighted from a handsome black pony a very dignified person.

  (CATHY *is greeted by* HINDLEY.)

HINDLEY Why, Cathy, you are quite a beauty. I should scarcely have known you!

CATHY E Is Heathcliff not here?

HINDLEY Heathcliff! You may come and wish Miss Catherine welcome like the other servants.

  (HEATHCLIFF *steps forward.*)

CATHY E How very black and cross you look! And how –

how funny and grim! But that's because I'm used to Edgar and Isabella Linton. Heathcliff, have you forgotten me?

HEATHCLIFF   I thought you'd forgotten me.

HINDLEY   Shake hands, Heathcliff. Once in a while that is permitted.

HEATHCLIFF   I shan't stand to be laughed at.

CATHY E   I didn't mean to laugh at you. I couldn't help myself. Heathcliff, shake hands, at least! What are you sulky for? It was only that you looked odd. If you wash your face and brush your hair, it will be all right. But you are so dirty!

HEATHCLIFF   You needn't have touched me! I'll be dirty as I please.

              (*He dashes away and goes to sit.*)

CATHY E   Why is Heathcliff like this?

HINDLEY   Let him stay away. Mrs Linton has begged that he be kept apart from her little darlings.

CATHY E   But I want him to join in. We'll have such fun; carols and mulled wine . . .

HINDLEY   Heathcliff's not like us. Come, let's find Frances and you can help her plan the day.

              (ACTOR 5 *starts to sing "Ding Dong Merrily On High." The others join in. At the end all applaud politely.* ACTORS 2 *and* 3 *go to sit.* ACTOR 5 *brings a chair forward for* HEATHCLIFF.)

ACTOR 5   In the morning Heathcliff rose early and carried his ill-humour onto the moors, not reappearing until the family were departed for church.

HEATHCLIFF   Nelly, make me decent, I'm going to be good.

NELLY	You have grieved Catherine, she's sorry she ever came home.
HEATHCLIFF	Did she say she was grieved?
NELLY	She's cried.
HEATHCLIFF	So have I. And I had more reason than she.

(*She begins to smooth his hair, etc.*)

NELLY	You are younger, yet taller and twice as broad as Edgar Linton and could knock him down in a twinkling.
HEATHCLIFF	If I knocked him down twenty times that wouldn't make him less handsome. I wish I had light hair and fair skin, and had a chance of being rich.
NELLY	Oh, you're showing poor spirit. You're fit for a prince in disguise. Who knows but your father was Emperor of China and your mother an Indian queen, each of them able to buy up, with one week's income, Wuthering Heights and Thrushcross Grange together. And you were kidnapped by wicked sailors and brought to England. Frame high notions of your birth and let it give you courage.
CATHY E	(*off*) The Lintons are here!
NELLY	Remember, show your good humour.

(*Exit* NELLY *to sit. Voices: "Come in, come in! Welcome! Merry Christmas", etc.* HINDLEY *enters, followed by* EDGAR *and* CATHY.)

HINDLEY	Why, Heathcliff! You vagabond, we don't want you cramming your fingers in the tarts, do we? Wait till I get hold of those elegant locks – see if I won't pull them a bit longer.
EDGAR	They are long enough already. I wonder they don't make his head ache.

HEATHCLIFF	For the love of . . . !
	(HEATHCLIFF *moves to strike* EDGAR *but is stopped by* HINDLEY.)
HINDLEY	Go to your room. I'll deal with you there. Go to your room!
	(HEATHCLIFF *goes to sit on upstage side of window seat.*)
CATHY E	You should not have spoken to him! He was already in a bad temper and now you've spoilt your visit, and he'll be flogged. I hate him to be flogged. Why did you speak to him?
EDGAR	I promised mama that I wouldn't say one word to him and I didn't!
CATHY E	Well. don't cry. You're not killed.
HINDLEY	Next time, Master Edgar, take the law into your own fists – it will give you an appetite! Come, let's join the others.
	(*Music.*)
ACTOR 3	Hindley carved bountiful platefuls and in the evening they were joined by the Gimmerton band – trumpets, clarinets, French horns . . .
	(*Still sitting, the* ACTORS *make polite conversation as if talking to other guests.* HINDLEY *sits downstage as if smoking a cigar.*)
CATHY E	Hindley, please let Heathcliff come down.
HINDLEY	No!
CATHY E	If we dance Isabella will have no partner.
HINDLEY	She can dance with me.
CATHY E	You have Frances.

HINDLEY   Frances is resting, it's been a tiring day.

CATHY E   She won't want to dance with you.

HINDLEY   And she won't want to dance with Heathcliff.

CATHY E   Well, none of us shall dance then. I shall sit at the
                 top of the stairs and listen.

                 (*Laughter from the other actors.*)

ACTOR 2   No one noticed Cathy's absence, for the house was
                 so full of people. She didn't stay at the top of the
                 stairs but climbed to the garret where she could
                 whisper to Heathcliff through the boards . . .

                 (ACTOR 2 *sits on downstage side of window seat
                 adjacent to* HEATHCLIFF.)

CATHY E   Heathcliff! Heathcliff!

HEATHCLIFF   Leave me alone.

CATHY E   Talk to me.

HEATHCLIFF   I've nothing to say.

CATHY E   Listen, the music's so lovely. If only we could
                 dance!

HEATHCLIFF   We could.

CATHY E   How?

HEATHCLIFF   Go to the next garret, and out of the skylight . . .

CATHY E   I can run along the roof and you can let me in!

ACTOR 2   Cathy was afraid of nothing and despite the wind
                 and the cold night she was soon in the room.

                 (HEATHCLIFF *stands on the window seat.* CATHY
                 climbs to join him. He catches her in his arms.)

HEATHCLIFF	Shh!
CATHY E	Hold me around the waist and take my hand.
	(*They hold each other and move slowly to the music.* NELLY *approaches as if calling through the door.*)
NELLY	Miss Cathy! I know what you're up to. Come out, someone will hear you!
CATHY E	Take Heathcliff to the kitchen, give him some food.
NELLY	I can't, he'll be found.
HEATHCLIFF	I'm not hungry. I'm trying to settle how I shall pay Hindley back.
NELLY	It is for God to punish wicked people; we should learn to forgive.
HEATHCLIFF	God won't have the satisfaction that I shall.
ACTOR 4	Over the next six months Cathy kept up her acquaintance with the Lintons.
ACTOR 2	But she never stopped loving Heathcliff and spent as many wild days on the moors as she did at Thrushcross Grange.
	(*Music fades.* ACTORS 1 *and* 2 *freeze.*)
ACTOR 3	Hindley paid them little attention; he had other things on his mind: his wife, heavy with child, grew weak with consumption by the day.
	(ACTOR 5 *becomes* FRANCES. *She coughs heavily and stumbles across the stage, leaning on an umbrella.*)
	And although the baby was born healthy . . .
ACTOR 5	. . . the doctor announced . . .

Actor 4	(*stepping forward*) . . . that his mother had nothing to keep her now and would be dead before the winter.
Hindley	Damn the doctor!
Actor 4	(*as* Doctor) You should have known better than to choose such a rush of a lass.
Hindley	She'll be well by this time next week.
Actor 4	The winter will finish her.
Hindley	She's stronger already. She was never in consumption.
Actor 4	And medicine is useless.
Hindley	She needs no medicine.
Actor 4	Tomorrow she will be dead!
	(Actor 5 *puts up the umbrella and gives it to* Actor 3.)
Hindley	Frances . . . Frances . . . NO!!!!
	(*He walks forward with the umbrella.*)
Actor 3	Hindley's child was named Hareton, and he fell wholly into the hands of Nelly Dean the housekeeper. Hindley never wept, nor prayed, but he cursed and defied.
	(Actor 3 *puts down the umbrella and goes to sit.*)
Actor 1	His anger was taken out on Heathcliff.
	(Actor 1 *goes to sit.*)
Actor 4	Edgar Linton seldom visited Wuthering Heights. He had a terror of Earnshaw's reputation.
	(Actor 4 *goes to sit.*)

(ACTOR 2 *steps down from window.*)

ACTOR 2   But Catherine was full of ambition, and when Hindley had gone from home one afternoon she managed to inform Edgar of his absence and was soon preparing to receive him.

(ACTOR 5 *freezes in the motion of cleaning the window.* HEATHCLIFF *approaches* CATHY.)

HEATHCLIFF   Are you going out?

CATHY E   No, it's raining.

HEATHCLIFF   Why are you dressed up? Is somebody coming?

CATHY E   Not that I know of . . . you should be in the field now.

HEATHCLIFF   Hindley's away. I'll not work any more today, I'll stay with you. We can take a picnic.

CATHY E   Someone will tell . . .

(NELLY *breaks from the freeze.*)

NELLY   Not me, miss.

(NELLY *freezes again.*)

CATHY E   Edgar Linton talked of calling this afternoon. As it rains I hardly expect him; but he may come, and if he does, you run the risk of being scolded for no good reason.

HEATHCLIFF   Don't turn me out for those pitiful friends of yours!

CATHY E   What are you saying?

HEATHCLIFF   If you look at the calendar in the kitchen it's marked with dots and crosses – the crosses are for the evenings you have spent with the Lintons. The dots for those spent with me. There are a lot more crosses.

CATHY E	As if I took notice. Where is the sense in that?
HEATHCLIFF	To show that I do take notice.
CATHY E	And should I always be sitting with you? What do you talk about? You don't read.
HEATHCLIFF	I can read, you know that, but I've no longer any books.
CATHY E	Take mine, then. You had only to ask.
HEATHCLIFF	You never told me before that you disliked my company.
CATHY E	It is no company when people know nothing and say nothing.

(ACTOR 4 *rises and enters as* EDGAR.)

EDGAR	I'm not come too soon, am I?
HEATHCLIFF	(*whisper*) Better that you never came at all.

(HEATHCLIFF *goes to sit.*)

EDGAR	Such a vulgar ruffian . . .
CATHY E	He knows nothing else!
EDGAR	You don't belong here, Catherine! Not any more!
CATHY E	And where do I belong?
EDGAR	At the Grange.
CATHY E	You mean you miss me?
EDGAR	Of course!
CATHY	And I miss the library and the cakes.

(*Laughter. Then, noticing* NELLY . . .)

Why don't you go to my room, Nelly, and get Heathcliff the books he so craves?

NELLY   But I'm busy here, Miss.

CATHY E   I hate you to be fidgeting.

(CATHY *physically tries to extract her, then nips her.*)

Now, do as I say.

NELLY   You have no right to nip me and I'm not going to bear it!

CATHY E   I didn't touch you, you lying creature.

NELLY   You're the liar, miss . . .

(CATHY *slaps* NELLY *on the cheek. Again, it is a stylised slap – there is no physical contact.*)

EDGAR   Catherine! Catherine!

CATHY E   (*to* NELLY) Leave the room !

(NELLY *moves towards the upstage of the window, nursing her cheek.* ACTOR 4 *attempts to leave.*)

CATHY E   (*to* EDGAR) You must not go.

EDGAR   I must and shall.

CATHY E   Sit down, you shall not leave me in that temper. I should be miserable all night, and I won't be miserable for you!

EDGAR   How can I stay? You've made me afraid and ashamed of you. I'll not come here again.

CATHY E   Well, go if you please – get away! And now I'll cry – I'll cry myself sick!

NELLY	Miss is dreadfully wayward, sir! As bad as any marred child – you'd better be riding home.
EDGAR	Don't cry. Don't cry, please, Catherine. Everything is going to be alright.

(*They go to sit as* ACTOR 3 *steps forward as* HINDLEY. *He carries a knife.*)

ACTOR 3	Hindley Earnshaw had returned in a rage, as he would do on many an occasion. He would seek out his shotgun, find it empty of lead and search desperately for his son Hareton.

(ACTOR 5 *has picked up a shawl which she uses to represent a young child in her arms.*)

ACTOR 5	Mrs Dean would often hide the child for fear of it being kissed to death or flung into the fire . . .
ACTOR 4	. . . depending on Hindley's mood!
HINDLEY	By Heaven and Hell, where's my child? I want to see him. I know you've sworn between you to murder it!

(EDGAR *and* CATHY *sit.*)

ACTOR 4	Hindley's arrival drove Linton speedily to his horse.
ACTOR 2	And Catherine to follow him.
ACTOR 3	Where's that bairn? I want my son, Mrs Dean!

(NELLY *steps forward as if cradling a child.*)

ACTOR 3	I know how you are, always making sure he's out of my way.
NELLY	You're in no fit state.
HINDLEY	Give him to me or I swear I'll kill you!

(HINDLEY *threatens* NELLY *with the knife.*)

NELLY   I don't like the carving knife, it's been cutting red
              herrings. I'd rather be shot if you please.

HINDLEY   You'd rather be damned!

              (*He takes the baby from* NELLY.)

HINDLEY   Hush child, hush. Kiss me, kiss me, Hareton,
              damn thee! Be sure as I'm living I'll break the brat's
              neck . . .

NELLY   Mr Earnshaw, please . . .

              (*He climbs onto the window seat.*)

ACTOR 3   He carried the child upstairs and lifted him dangling
              over the bannister.

              (ACTORS 2 *and* 4 *catch their breath.* ACTOR 1 *moves
              to take up a position below* HINDLEY, *facing him.*)

ACTOR 1   But on hearing a noise below he leaned over the
              rails to listen . . .

HINDLEY   Who's that?

ACTOR 5   The baby gave a sudden spring . . . releasing himself
              from the grasp that held him, and fell!

              (*All other actors let out a cry, as if watching the
              baby fall. In slow motion, the shawl* [*baby*] *is
              transferred from* HINDLEY *to* HEATHCLIFF.)

ACTOR 3   But at that critical moment Heathcliff arrived
              underneath and caught him!

ACTOR 1   It was a natural impulse. Looking up and seeing
              Hindley he realised that he had thwarted his own
              revenge.

              (*Music.* ACTOR 3 *goes to sit.* HEATHCLIFF *puts the
              shawl around* NELLY *then moves as if to exit, but
              stays in the shadows behind the window to listen.*

NELLY *is still nursing her slapped cheek.* ACTOR 2 *moves forward.*)

CATHY E   Nelly, will you keep a secret?

NELLY   Is it worth keeping?

CATHY E   . . . Edgar Linton asked me to marry him!

NELLY   I see.

CATHY E   And I've given him an answer!

NELLY   Considering the exhibition you performed in his presence this afternoon, I might say it would be wise to refuse him – since he asked you after that, he must be hopelessly stupid.

CATHY E   If you talk so I won't tell you any more – I accepted him. Be quick and say whether I was wrong.

NELLY   What good is it discussing the matter? You have pledged your word and cannot retract.

CATHY E   But say whether I should have done so.

NELLY   Do you love him?

CATHY E   Of course I do.

NELLY   Why do you love him?

CATHY E   I do – that's sufficient.

NELLY   You must say why.

CATHY E   Because he is handsome and pleasant to be with.

NELLY   Bad!

CATHY E   Because he is young and cheerful.

NELLY   Bad still.

CATHY E   Because he loves me.

NELLY   Indifferent, coming there.

CATHY E   And he will be rich, and I shall like to be the greatest
                woman of the neighbourhood!

NELLY   Worst of all! And now say how you love him?

CATHY E   You're making a jest of it.

NELLY   You love Mr Edgar, because he is handsome, and
                young and cheerful, and rich, and he loves you! But
                there are other handsome, rich men in the world.

CATHY E   I have seen none like Edgar.

NELLY   But you may see some. He will not always be
                handsome and young and he may not always be
                rich.

CATHY E   He is now and I have only to do with the present.

NELLY   Well, that settles it – if you have only to do with the
                present, then marry Mr Linton.

CATHY E   I shall.

NELLY   Then where is the obstacle?

CATHY E   Here! And here! (*She strikes her forehead and her
                breast.*) In whichever place the soul lives – in my
                soul and in my heart I'm convinced I'm wrong.

NELLY   That's very strange.

CATHY E   Do you never dream queer dreams? I've dreamt in
                my life dreams that have stayed with me ever after,
                and have changed my ideas; they've gone through
                and through me, like wine through water, and altered
                the colour of my mind.

NELLY   We're dismal enough without conjuring up ghosts
                and visions to perplex us.

CATHY E   I dreamt once that I was in Heaven and I was miserable.

NELLY   Because you're not fit to go there. All sinners would be miserable in Heaven.

CATHY E   It didn't seem my home; and I broke my heart with weeping to come back to earth; and the angels were so angry that they flung me out, into the middle of the heath, on the top of Wuthering Heights, where I woke sobbing for joy. You see, that explains it! I've no more business to marry Edgar Linton than I have to be in Heaven. But it would degrade me to marry Heathcliff now, so he shall never know I love him; and that's not because he's handsome, but because he's more myself than I am. Whatever our souls are made of, his and mine are the same, and Linton's as different as frost from fire.

(They become aware of HEATHCLIFF'S *presence. He moves.)*

NELLY   Shhh.

CATHY E   Did he hear me? Even if he did, he wouldn't understand, would he? He does not know what being in love is.

NELLY   Why should he not know as well as you? Have you considered how you'll bear the separation and how he'll bear to be deserted in the world?

CATHY E   Who is to separate us? Not as long as I live. That's not what I mean. He'll be as much to me as he has been all his lifetime. Edgar must tolerate him. He will when he learns my true feelings towards him. If Heathcliff and I married we would be beggars; if I marry Linton I can aid Heathcliff to rise and place him out of my brother's power.

NELLY   With your husband's money? That's the worst motive you've given yet for being Linton's wife.

CATHY E No, it's for the best! My love for Heathcliff is like the eternal rocks – a source of little visible delight, but necessary. I am Heathcliff – he's always, always in my mind – not as a pleasure, any more than I am always a pleasure to myself – but as my own being! Promise, promise to keep my secret.

NELLY No, I won't!

CATHY E Promise!

NELLY What does it matter? He heard a good part of what you said anyway.

CATHY E Heathcliff! What did I say to grieve him? Heathcliff!

NELLY He'll be on the moors by now.

CATHY E Heathcliff! He was already vexed at my bad humour this afternoon. I'll wait by the gate.

NELLY It's raining.

CATHY E Then I'll get wet!

(*Other* ACTORS *make noise of wind.*)

ACTOR 2 By midnight the storm was rattling over the Heights in full fury and Cathy got thoroughly drenched through, wandering bonnet-less and shawl-less to and fro from the gate to the door. (*As* CATHY.) Heathcliff!!!!

NELLY Come to bed; there's no use waiting longer on that foolish boy.

(ACTOR 5 *goes to sit.*)

CATHY E Heathcliff!!!

(*Lights. Music.*)

ACTOR 4 The next morning sunbeams pierced the chinks of the shutters and Catherine, having been up all night, shivered near the fireplace.

HINDLEY	What ails you? Why are you so damp and pale?
CATHY E	I'm cold.
HINDLEY	What kept you up? Not fear of thunder?
CATHY E	Shut the window. I'm starving.
HINDLEY	You're ill. Damn it! I don't want to be troubled with more sickness. What took you into the rain? Heathcliff?
CATHY E	He's gone. (*She weeps, inconsolable with grief.*) He's gone!!!
HINDLEY	Stop snivelling and get to your room!
CATHY E	He's gone . . . Heathcliff has gone . . . !

(*Music.* CATHY *weeps then gradually the tears turn to a false kind of laughter as* CATHY, EDGAR *and* NELLY *form a wedding tableau in front of the window frame.* NELLY *passes* CATHY *a small bunch of heather.* ACTOR 3 *becomes a Victorian photographer and mimes taking a photograph.*)

ACTOR 3	It was a small wedding party. Old Mr and Mrs Linton had both died and Hindley was too drunk to attend. There was no honeymoon either, no great celebration; after the wedding they returned to Thrushcross Grange.
ACTOR 5	Despite her reluctance to leave Hareton, Nelly was persuaded to accompany them, and was surprised to see Cathy settle in so well.
ACTOR 2	She seemed almost over-fond of Mr Linton and even his sister, Isabella.

(ACTOR 5 *giggles as* ACTOR 2 *passes her the heather.*)

ACTOR 4   Although Edgar had a deep-rooted fear of ruffling
             her humour, for she had seasons of gloom and
             silence.

ACTOR 2   Nevertheless over the years they seemed in
             possession of a deep and growing happiness.

ACTOR 1   But that would end on a shadowy, mellow evening
             one September:

             (*Music. Lights.* CATHY *and* ISABELLA *sit. Enter*
             ACTOR 3 *as* MANSERVANT.)

ACTOR 3   (*to* CATHY E) A gentleman from Gimmerton wishes to
             see you ma'am.

CATHY E   What does he want?

ACTOR 3   I didn't question him.

EDGAR   Then show him in!

             (HEATHCLIFF *enters. He has changed. He looks*
             dignified and has been educated.)

CATHY E   (*stunned*) Heathcliff ... Oh Edgar, Edgar darling,
             look who's come back!

EDGAR   There's no need to be frantic.

             (HEATHCLIFF *very slowly kisses* CATHY'S *hand.*)

CATHY E   But I'm so happy and now we must all be friends, for
             my sake.

EDGAR   Try to be glad without being absurd then. Sir ... sit
             down. Mrs Linton would have me give you a cordial
             reception and, of course, I am gratified when
             anything occurs to please her.

HEATHCLIFF   And I also.

             (ACTOR 3 *brings* HEATHCLIFF *a chair then exits to*
             sit. HEATHCLIFF *sits opposite* CATHY. *They are*

absorbed in each other. Cathy *is almost breathless.*)

CATHY E   I shall think it a dream tomorrow. I shall not be able to believe that I have seen and touched and spoken to you once more . . .

EDGAR   Mr Heathcliff will have a long walk wherever he may lodge tonight; and we should . . .

HEATHCLIFF   I'm staying at Wuthering Heights. Mr Earnshaw invited me when I called this morning.

CATHY E   Hindley invited you?

(ACTOR 3, *from where he is sitting at the back, mimes playing poker.*)

HEATHCLIFF   I offered liberal payment.

CATHY E   He was always greedy.

ISABELLA   You shall be within a short distance then?

HEATHCLIFF   Yes.

EDGAR   I see.

CATHY E   Look at you, all changed and . . . where have you been?

HEATHCLIFF   You must visit me.

CATHY E   Tomorrow, we'll come tomorrow . . .

EDGAR   I have business in Gimmerton tomorrow.

CATHY E   Then I'll go with Isabella.

ISABELLA   Oh yes!

CATHY E   If you don't mind?

EDGAR   (*a beat*) No, I don't mind! Now, it's time for supper, so we must bid you goodnight, Mr Heathcliff.

HEATHCLIFF   Of course.

                (HEATHCLIFF *moves to go.* CATHY *rises and moves towards him.*)

CATHY E   (*whispers*) I have endured such misery because of you.

HEATHCLIFF   And I because of you . . .

ISABELLA   Let me show you out, sir . . .

                (*Exit* HEATHCLIFF *and* ISABELLA *to form a tableau behind the window.*)

CATHY E   Oh Edgar, I am so happy!

EDGAR   Please, Catherine . . .

CATHY E   You are the most wonderful husband . . .

EDGAR   Leave me, I am sick and sleepy.

                (*He exits to sit. Fade up music.*)

ACTOR 1   Heathcliff used the liberty of visiting the Grange cautiously.

                (ACTOR 1 *goes to sit.*)

ACTOR 2   Catherine also deemed it judicious to moderate her expressions of pleasure in receiving him; and he gradually established his right to be expected.

ACTOR 4   Edgar's uneasiness experienced a lull but there was soon a new source of trouble . . .

ACTOR 5   Isabella Linton, a charming young lady now of eighteen – infantile in manners, though possessed of a keen wit and temper, grew cross and wearisome with regard to Mr Heathcliff!

(ACTORS 2 *and* 5 *become* CATHY *and* ISABELLA.)

CATHY E   If you're not well, Isabella, I'll send for the doctor.

ISABELLA   My health is perfect, it is your harshness that makes
               me unhappy.

CATHY E   When have I been harsh?

ISABELLA   Yesterday in our walk along the moor, you told me
               to ramble where I pleased, while you sauntered on
               with Mr Heathcliff.

CATHY E   Then I'll repeat our conversation word for word and
               you point out any charm it could have for you.

ISABELLA   I don't mind the conversation. I wanted to be with
               him, and I won't be always sent off.

CATHY E   I hope I have misunderstood you, Isabella.

ISABELLA   No, you have not. I love him more than you ever
               loved Edgar, and he might love me if you would let
               him!

CATHY E   Love him? Don't imagine that he conceals depths of
               benevolence and affection. He's not a rough
               diamond – he's a fierce, pitiless, wolfish man and
               he'd crush you like a sparrow's egg.

ISABELLA   For shame!

CATHY E   And I know he couldn't love a Linton and yet he'd
               be quite capable of marrying your fortune.

ISABELLA   You are worse than twenty foes.

CATHY E   You think I speak from wicked selfishness?

ISABELLA   I'm certain you do. He must have an honourable
               soul or he would not have remembered you!

(HEATHCLIFF *approaches.*)

HEATHCLIFF   Ladies . . .

CATHY E   Here are two people sadly in need of a third to thaw
                    the ice between them. Heathcliff, I'm proud to show
                    you, at last, somebody that dotes on you more than
                    myself – my poor little sister-in-law is breaking her
                    heart by mere contemplation of your physical and
                    moral beauty. It lies in your own power to be
                    Edgar's brother.

                    (ISABELLA *tries to leave.*)

                    No, no, Isabella, you shan't run off.

                    (CATHY *grabs her arm and holds her tight.*)

                    She is to shoot a shaft into your soul that would fix
                    you forever and send my image into eternal
                    oblivion!

ISABELLA   I'd thank you to adhere to the truth. What amuses
                    you is painful to me beyond expression.

                    (HEATHCLIFF *says nothing.*)

CATHY E   Why don't you show more pleasure at such news?
                    She has fasted ever since the day-before-
                    yesterday's walk, from sorrow and rage that I
                    despatched her out of your society.

HEATHCLIFF   She wishes to be out of my society now at any rate.

                    (ISABELLA *tries to get away from* CATHY *by digging
                    in her nails.*)

CATHY E   There's a tigress! Begone for God's sake and hide
                    your vixen face!

                    (*Exit* ISABELLA *to sit upstage.*)

HEATHCLIFF   What did you mean by teasing the creature in that
                    manner?

CATHY E	I like her too well to let you absolutely devour her up.
HEATHCLIFF	And I like her too ill to attempt it. If I lived alone with that mawkish waxen face . . . She detestably resembles Linton. She's her brother's heir, is she not?
CATHY E	No, it is a male heir that would inherit.
HEATHCLIFF	Her sons then?
CATHY E	Not before mine! And mine shall be born in the spring.
HEATHCLIFF	(*a beat*) You're with child?
CATHY E	Yes!
HEATHCLIFF	Yet still you torture me.
CATHY E	I can't deny Edgar.
HEATHCLIFF	You may have a daughter.
CATHY E	You are too prone to covet your neighbour's goods – remember this neighbour's goods are mine.
	(ACTOR 2 *goes to sit.*)
ACTOR 1	Heathcliff had not the habit of bestowing a single unnecessary civility on Miss Linton. But knowing her secret, swore he'd make the most of it.
ACTOR 5	Isabella had not spoken to her sister-in-law for three days and had developed the habit of taking herself into the garden where she would sit alone and read.
	(ACTOR 5 *becomes* ISABELLA. *She sits reading.* HEATHCLIFF *approaches.*)
HEATHCLIFF	So you wish to spend more time with me, Miss Linton?

ISABELLA	No, I . . .
HEATHCLIFF	Oh! You were lying, then?
ISABELLA	Please, I . . .
HEATHCLIFF	Shh!

(*He kisses her. She tears away, upset.* ACTORS 2, 3 *and* 4 *stand as if shocked by* HEATHCLIFF'S *boldness. They also take a sharp intake of breath.* ACTOR 2 *approaches* HEATHCLIFF, *the others sit back down.*)

CATHY E	I said you must let Isabella alone!
HEATHCLIFF	Yes, you did!
CATHY E	Unless you are tired of being received here and wish Edgar to draw the bolts against you!
HEATHCLIFF	God forbid that he should try.
CATHY E	Don't vex me.
HEATHCLIFF	I have a right to kiss her and you have no right to object – I'm not your husband, you needn't be jealous of me!
CATHY E	I'm not jealous of you. If you like Isabella you shall marry her. But do you like her? Tell the truth.
HEATHCLIFF	You tell the truth about how you have treated me! And if you flatter yourself that I don't perceive it, you are a fool – I'll not suffer unrevenged.
CATHY E	Unrevenged?
HEATHCLIFF	Not on you! You're welcome to torture me to death for your amusement, only allow me to amuse myself a little in the same style. If I imagined you really wished me to marry Isabella I'd cut my throat.
CATHY E	Oh, the evil is that I am not jealous is it? Well, quarrel with Edgar if you please and deceive his

sister and you'll have hit on exactly the best method
of revenging yourself on me!

HEATHCLIFF   Why did you do it?

CATHY E   For you . . . for . . .

HEATHCLIFF   (*raising voice*) You did it for yourself, Catherine
Earnshaw! For yourself!

(EDGAR *enters.*)

EDGAR   I'll not have this talk, not to my wife.

(HEATHCLIFF *laughs.*)

I have been so far forbearing with you, sir, not that I
was ignorant of your miserable character, but I felt
that you were only partly responsible for that. Your
presence here is a moral poison that would
contaminate the most virtuous. I shall deny you,
hereafter, admission to this house, and give notice
that I require your instant departure.

HEATHCLIFF   This lamb of yours threatens like a bull. It is in
danger of splitting it's skull against my knuckles. By
God, Edgar Linton, I'm mortally sorry that you are
not worth knocking down.

EDGAR   Well, I really . . .

(EDGAR *is taken with nervous trembling and leans
on the back of a chair.*)

CATHY E   Oh Heavens, Edgar! Heathcliff would as soon lift a
finger at you as the King would march his army
against a colony of mice.

HEATHCLIFF   (*to* CATHY) I wish you joy of the milk-blooded
coward! I compliment you on your taste, and that is
the slavering, shivering thing you preferred to me! Is
he weeping or is he going to faint from fear?

(EDGAR *strikes* HEATHCLIFF, *again with no actual physical contact. It causes* HEATHCLIFF *to choke.* EDGAR *goes to sit.*)

CATHY E   You've done with coming here now. Get away – he'll return with a brace of pistols. If he did overhear us, he'd never forgive you. You've played me an ill turn. Go! I'd rather see Edgar suffer than you.

HEATHCLIFF   Do you suppose I'm going with that blow burning in my gullet? If I don't floor him now I shall murder him!

CATHY E   He'll call the gardeners and coachman who'll all have bludgeons. Go!

HEATHCLIFF   I shall murder him!

CATHY E   Go!

(HEATHCLIFF *kisses* CATHY, *then makes his escape. He goes to sit.* EDGAR *returns.*)

EDGAR   Cathy . . .

CATHY E   They'll never catch him!

EDGAR   Cathy?

CATHY E   Oh, for God's sake!

EDGAR   Please . . . I am neither come to wrangle nor be reconciled, I just wish to learn . . .

CATHY E   What?

EDGAR   Will you give up Heathcliff hereafter? It is impossible for you to be his friend and my wife, and I absolutely require to know which you choose!

CATHY E   I require to be let alone. I demand it! Don't you see how upset I am with it all? I can scarcely stand! Edgar, you . . . you leave me! Nelly!

(*She becomes breathless. She is making herself ill. Enter* ACTOR 5 *as* NELLY.)

EDGAR   Cathy! (*To* NELLY.) Fetch some water!

NELLY   There's nothing the matter.

EDGAR   Of course there is. See how pale she's gone?

NELLY   She has had this planned.

(CATHY *glares at* NELLY *then rushes away to sit on the window seat facing upstage.*)

EDGAR   Catherine! Catherine, please!

ACTOR 5   She ran to her room and locked herself in.

EDGAR   Catherine, please!

(*Music.* ACTOR 4 *goes to sit.*)

ACTOR 5   The next morning she never appeared at breakfast and when asked if she would have some carried up she replied:

CATHY E   No!

ACTOR 3   The same question was repeated at dinner, and tea; and again on the day after, and received the same answer:

CATHY E   No, no, no!

ACTOR 1   Having taken Nelly's advice, Mr Linton spent his time in the library, and did not inquire concerning his wife's occupations.

(ACTOR 1 *presents* ACTOR 4 *with a book then goes to sit.*)

ACTOR 4   But he did speak to his sister, giving her solemn warning that if she were so insane as to encourage that worthless suitor, it would dissolve all bonds of relationship between herself and him.

(ACTOR 4 *goes to sit. Music.* ACTORS 3 *and* 1 *bring the window downstage.* CATHY *follows and sits on the window seat as music fades under.*)

CATHY E   I need a new pitcher of water! I will die since no one cares anything about me. Edgar does not love me at all – he would never miss me! Has he fallen into lethargy, or is he dead?

NELLY   Mr Linton is tolerably well, he is continually among his books.

CATHY E   His books! And I on the brink of the grave! My God! Does he know how I'm altered?

NELLY   He has no idea of you being deranged and he does not fear that you will let yourself die of hunger!

CATHY E   For three awful nights I've never closed my lids – I've been tormented! What in the name of all that feels has he to do with books, when I am dying? Open the window, I'm too hot.

NELLY   It's the middle of winter!

CATHY E   Open the window!

(NELLY *mimes opening the window.* ACTORS 1, 3 *and* 4 *make the sound of the wind.*)

CATHY E   This room is haunted! If I were in my own bed in the old house! And that wind wounding in the firs by the lattice. Do let me feel it – it comes straight down the moor – do let me have one breath!

NELLY   Stop this! Lie down and shut your eyes.

CATHY E   Do you know what has been recurring in my head as I lay there . . . it is as if the whole last seven years of my life has been a blank and I have just awoken here wrenched from the Heights and Heathcliff and converted at a stroke into Mrs Linton, the wife of a stranger! An exile, an outcast; grovelling in an abyss! I wish I was a girl again, half savage and hardy and free . . . laughing at injuries, not maddening under them! Why am I so changed? I'm sure I should be myself were I among the heather. Open the window again wide!

NELLY   You'll catch your death!

(Wind noises stop immediately. Music out.)

ACTOR 3   There was no moon that night; everything lay in misty darkness. Not a light beamed from any house!

(CATHY climbs to stand on the seat, looking out.)

CATHY E   Look! That's my room with the candle in it and the trees swaying before it. You're waiting till I come home that you may lock the gate. You'll wait a while yet; it's a rough journey and a sad heart to travel it and we must pass by Gimmeton Kirk. We've braved its ghosts often together, Heathcliff and I, and dared each other to stand among the graves and ask them to come. But Heathcliff, if I dare you now, will you venture? If you do, I'll keep you. I'll not lie there by myself; they may bury me twelve feet deep, and throw the church down over me, but I won't rest till you are with me. I never will. He's considering . . . he'd rather I'd come to him. Be content, you always followed me!

(EDGAR enters.)

NELLY   Sir! The mistress is ill. She's eaten scarcely anything!

CATHY E   You are come are you, Edgar Linton? You are one of those things that are ever found when least wanted, and when you are wanted, never!

EDGAR   Cathy?

CATHY E	I suppose we shall have plenty of lamentations now . . . but they can't keep me from my narrow home out yonder where I am bound before spring is over! There it is, not among the Lintons, mind, under the chapel roof, but in the open air with a headstone, and you may please yourself whether you go to them or come to me !
EDGAR	Am I nothing to you any more? Do you love Heathcliff?
CATHY E	You mention that name and I end the matter, instantly, by a spring from the window.
EDGAR	Cathy?
CATHY E	I don't want you, Edgar; I'm past wanting you; return to your books . . .
NELLY	Her mind wanders, sir. She has been talking nonsense the whole evening. But let her have quiet and she'll rally.
EDGAR	I desire no further advise from you, Mrs Dean. You knew her nature and encouraged me to harass her!
	(ACTOR 3 enters as SERVANT.)
ACTOR 3	Master, master! Miss Isabella . . .
EDGAR	Speak lower, what is the matter?
ACTOR 3	She's gone! Run off with Mr Heathcliff!
	(CATHY collapses on to the seat.)
EDGAR	What?
ACTOR 3	Should we try any measures for bringing her back?
EDGAR	No. Trouble me no more about her; hereafter she is only my sister in name, not because I disown her but because she has disowned me.

(ACTOR 5 *sings verse of "Did You Not Hear My Lady." ACTORS 3 and 4 return the window upstage centre.*)

ACTOR 5   (*sings*) Did you not hear My Lady
Go down the garden singing?
Blackbird and thrush were silent
To hear the alleys ringing . . .
Oh saw you not My Lady
Out in the garden there
Shaming the rose and lily
For she is twice as fair.

(*At the end of the song there is polite applause from the other actors. ACTORS 2 and 4 go to sit.*)

ACTOR 1   And on a dark evening about six weeks later Heathcliff finally brought his new wife back to Wuthering Heights. She was greeted by Hindley.

(ACTOR 1 *presents* ACTOR 3 *with a pistol then goes to sit.* ACTOR 5 *becomes* ISABELLA LINTON *and carries a carpet bag.*)

HINDLEY   What's your business here? Who are you?

ISABELLA   My name was Isabella Linton. You've seen me before, sir. I'm lately married to Mr Heathcliff and he has brought me here.

HINDLEY   Is he come back then?

ISABELLA   Yes, he left me by the kitchen door, for the doctor was passing and he wished to catch up with some news.

HINDLEY   It's well the hellish villain has kept his word.

ISABELLA   Your little boy wouldn't let me in and tried to frighten me off with a bulldog.

HINDLEY   His name is Hareton.

ISABELLA   Now, is there a maid that can show me to my room please? I'm tired with my journey.

HINDLEY   We have none, you must wait on yourself.

ISABELLA   Where must I sleep?

HINDLEY   Old Joseph will show you Heathcliff's chamber. Be so good as to turn your lock and draw your bolt. Look here! (HINDLEY *draws out the pistol.*) I go up with this every night and try his door. If I once find it open, he's done for. Not all the angels in Heaven shall save him. I don't care if you tell him – put him on his guard.

ISABELLA   Wouldn't it be wiser to bid him quit the house?

HINDLEY   And lose all without a chance of retrieval? Is Hareton to be a beggar?

ISABELLA   How so?

                (*Still in his seat,* ACTOR 1 *mimes playing poker.*)

HINDLEY   Gambling! I swear he has the hands of the Devil. He's taken all I own. But I will have it back and I'll have his gold too, then his blood, and Hell shall have his soul! Joseph!

ISABELLA   Why did you let him?

HINDLEY   Because I wanted all that was his. Joseph!

                (ACTOR 4 *enters as* JOSEPH, *an old Yorkshire farm hand.*)

ACTOR 4   Joseph, an old servant, entered. He was sinewy with a sour face and temperament to match. Sir . . .

ACTOR 3   Look here . . . Heathcliff's got himself a wife.

                (HINDLEY *exits, laughing.*)

JOSEPH	Good Lord! If aw mun hev a mistress set o'er me head, it's time tuh be flitting!
ISABELLA	I wish to see my bedroom.
JOSEPH	Bed rume! Maister Heathcliff allas keeps his locked un nob'dy iver mells on't but hisseln.
ISABELLA	But he's married now, and . . .
JOSEPH	You tackle him o'er it then.
ISABELLA	Well there are other rooms for Heaven's sake – let me settle somewhere!
JOSEPH	Tut tut, aw'm mista'en if ya shew yer sperrit lang. Will Heathcliff ide such bonny ways think ye?
	(*Enter* HEATHCLIFF.)
ISABELLA	You have the key to our room and . . .
HEATHCLIFF	It is not, nor will it ever be, our room. It is my room. I don't want you near me.
JOSEPH	I telled you.
	(JOSEPH *exits, laughing. He takes with him* ISABELLA'S *bag.*)
HEATHCLIFF	I have learnt just now that Cathy is gravely ill. It is your brother who has caused this and therefore you shall be his proxy in suffering until I get my hands on him . . .
ISABELLA	Oh!
HEATHCLIFF	I was a fool to fancy for a moment that she valued Edgar Linton's attachment more than mine – if he loved with all the powers of his puny being, he couldn't love in eighty years as much as I in one day.
ISABELLA	Heathcliff!

HEATHCLIFF He is scarcely a degree dearer to her than her dog, or a horse. It is not in him to be loved like me!

ISABELLA Catherine and Edgar are as fond of each other as any two people can be!

HEATHCLIFF Your brother is wondrous fond of you too! Yet he turns you adrift on the world!

ISABELLA He is not aware of what I suffer.

HEATHCLIFF The passion was wholly on one side. I never lied; it was idiocy to think that I could love you.

ISABELLA You are a devil! I know now that you married me to obtain power over my brother, but you shan't! I'll die first.

HEATHCLIFF Get upstairs!

ISABELLA And where will you go, to the Grange? They won't let you in. Cathy couldn't bear it.

HEATHCLIFF What she can't bear is being in isolation, with that insipid creature.

ISABELLA I won't hear my brother spoken of in that way.

HEATHCLIFF He might as well plant an oak in a flower pot and expect it to thrive, as imagine he can restore her to vigour in the soil of his shallow cares!

ISABELLA You'll get nowhere near her!

HEATHCLIFF I'll find a way! Now get upstairs.

(ACTOR 5 *goes to sit.*)

ACTOR 1 For the next two months Heathcliff haunted the garden of the Grange, waiting and watching.

ACTOR 2 Edgar tended Catherine day and night, sacrificing his own health and strength.

ACTOR 4   It was spring before her life was out of danger but
                as the winds turned soft again he rejoiced in the
                hope that she would soon return to her former self.

                (*Music.* ACTOR 2 *sits on window seat.* ACTOR 4 *puts a
                shawl over her. Music fades under.*)

CATHY E   Is the snow almost gone?

EDGAR   The snow is quite gone down here, darling. The sky
                is blue. Last spring at this time I was longing to
                have you under this roof. Now I wish you were a
                mile up those hills; the air blows so sweetly I feel
                that it would cure you.

CATHY   Next spring you'll long again to have me under this
                roof and you'll look back and think you were happy
                today.

EDGAR   Why don't you read a little?

CATHY E   I'm tired of being enclosed!

EDGAR   Look, the crocuses are out; sat here in the sunshine
                you could almost be outside . . .

                (*Enter* NELLY. CATHY *closes her eyes, resting.* NELLY
                whispers to EDGAR *across the frame of the window.*)

NELLY   Mr Linton . . .

EDGAR   What is it, Nelly?

NELLY   (*whisper*) I've received a letter from Miss Isabella.

EDGAR   (*a beat*) And?

NELLY   She says she's written to you and you've not
                replied! Sir, she begs that you send a token of
                forgiveness.

EDGAR   I have nothing to forgive her. You may go to
                Wuthering Heights and tell her that I'm not angry,

I'm sorry; sorry that I've lost her! But I shall not see her!

NELLY   Won't you write her a note?

EDGAR   Not as long as she is with Heathcliff.

(*Exit* EDGAR. CATHY *remains frozen.* ACTOR 3 *gives* ACTOR 5 *an umbrella.* ACTORS 3 *and* 4 *make wind noises.* NELLY *and* HEATHCLIFF *speak as if in a storm.* NELLY *struggles with the umbrella.*)

ACTOR 3   Edgar's coldness upset Nelly and on her way to the Heights she puzzled how to put heart into what Edgar had said of his sister.

NELLY   I would like to see Miss Isabella, sir!

HEATHCLIFF   She is delicate, as you know, and needs to rest.

NELLY   Treat her kindly.

HEATHCLIFF   Has her brother requested that?

NELLY   Her brother wishes her to have no contact as no good can come of it.

HEATHCLIFF   (*a beat*) How is Catherine?

NELLY   She'll never be like she was, but her life is spared.

HEATHCLIFF   You must get her to see me.

NELLY   Another encounter between you and the master would kill her altogether. She has nearly forgotten you.

HEATHCLIFF   You know she has not! You know as well as I do that for every thought she spends on Edgar, she spends a thousand on me. I only want to see how she is.

NELLY   She's restless and anxious.

HEATHCLIFF	Last night I was in the Grange garden, and I will return tonight and every night till I find an opportunity of entering.
NELLY	She couldn't bear it.
HEATHCLIFF	Then ask her! Ask her! She never mentions me because she daren't. You say she's restless – how could she not be in such isolation? She needs to see me, you know she does.
NELLY	No, you're wrong!
HEATHCLIFF	Be my friend, Nelly, as you have before. Let me know when Edgar is out. So I might come.
NELLY	(*a beat*) Come Sunday, Sunday is best.

(ACTOR 5 *puts down the umbrella. The wind dies as it blows* ACTORS 5 *and* 1 *back to sit and* ACTOR 4 *into position as* EDGAR.)

ACTOR 3	The Gimmerton bells rang out on that Sunday as they did every Sunday!

(EDGAR *is leaving for church.*)

EDGAR	Close your eyes and rest.
CATHY E	Must you go?
EDGAR	There's much to pray for! (*He touches her stomach.*) You've everything to look forward to.

(NELLY *enters.*)

Stoke up the fire, Nelly, and bring Mrs Linton some tea. (*He kisses* CATHY *tenderly.*) Keep warm, I won't be too long.

(*Exit* EDGAR *to sit.*)

CATHY E	No sugar, Nelly; I find it too sweet.

NELLY	(*a beat*) Mr Heathcliff is here! He wishes to see you whilst Mr Linton is out.
CATHY E	(*a beat*) Heathcliff . . . ?

(HEATHCLIFF *enters and immediately embraces* CATHY. *An intake of breath from the other actors.*)

HEATHCLIFF	Oh, Cathy! How can I bear it?

(CATHY *kisses* HEATHCLIFF. *He returns it. He then holds her and stares at her. He is hit with the realisation that she is going to die.*)

CATHY E	You and Edgar have broken my heart! And you both come to bewail the deed to me, as if you were the people to be pitied! How many years do you mean to live after I am gone?

(HEATHCLIFF *attempts to rise but* CATHY *holds onto him.*)

I wish I could hold you until we are both dead! Will you forget me – will you be happy when I am in the earth? Will you say twenty years hence, "That's the grave of Catherine Earnshaw; I loved her long ago, but I've loved many others since – my children are dearer to me than she was and, at death, I shall not rejoice that I am going to her. I shall be sorry that I must leave them!" Will you say so?

HEATHCLIFF	You lie to say I have killed you, and you know that I could as soon as forget you as my existence! While you are at peace, I shall be in Hell.
CATHY E	I shall not be at peace! I am not wishing you greater torment than I have, I only wish us never to be parted. You never harmed me in my life. If you nurse anger, that will be worse to remember than my harsh words!

(HEATHCLIFF *walks away from her. He does not want her to see his face which is raw with emotion.*)

See, you will not relent a moment to keep me out of the grave. That is how I am loved! That's not my Heathcliff. I shall love mine yet and take him with me – he's my soul!

HEATHCLIFF   Why did you betray your own heart? You loved me – what right had you to leave me? I have not broken your heart – you have broken it – and in breaking yours, you have broken mine!

CATHY E   If I've done wrong, I'm dying for it. Is it not enough? You left me too, but I forgive you. Forgive me!

HEATHCLIFF   Kiss me.

              (CATHY *and* HEATHCLIFF *are silent in each others' arms. Enter* NELLY.)

NELLY   Mr Heathcliff! Mrs Linton! Mr Linton is back already. I can see him at the gate!

HEATHCLIFF   I must go. But if I live I will see you again before you are asleep. I won't stray five yards from your window.

CATHY E   You can't go.

HEATHCLIFF   For one hour!

CATHY E   Not for one minute!

HEATHCLIFF   I must – Linton will be here.

              (CATHY *clings to him, not letting him go.*)

CATHY E   Don't, don't go. It is the last time! Heathcliff, I shall die! I shall die!

HEATHCLIFF   Hush. Hush. Ssh! Ssh!

              (EDGAR *enters.*)

EDGAR   What in Heavens . . . !

(HEATHCLIFF *breaks away.* CATHY *screams a piercing scream. Silence, then* ACTOR 4 *takes the shawl from her lap and holds it as if it is a baby.* CATHY *frozen.*)

ACTOR 5   At twelve o'clock that night a puny seven-month-old child was born.

ACTOR 3   And two hours later, the mother died, having never recovered consciousness.

HEATHCLIFF   No! May she wake in torment. Catherine Earnshaw, may you not rest as long as I am living! You said I killed you – haunt me then! *Haunt me*!

(ACTORS 3 *and* 5 *put up umbrellas.* ACTOR 2 *comes out of freeze and just sits.*)

ACTOR 5   Catherine's internment, to the surprise of the villagers, was neither in the Chapel nor under the carved monument of the Lintons.

ACTOR 3   Her grave was dug on the green slope, in a corner of the kirkyard where the wall is so low that heath and bilberry plants from the moor have climbed over it, and peat mould almost buries it.

CATHY E   Heathcliff!

ACTOR 5   (*sings*) It was just the time of eve
When parted ghosts might come
Above their prisoned dust to grieve
And wail their woeful doom.

CATHY E   Heathcliff.

(*Music – Haydn: All exit off stage.*)

END OF ACT ONE

ACT TWO

Same music as at the end of Act One. ACTORS *enter and assume same positions as at the end of Act One.*

HEATHCLIFF	Cathy! Cathy!
CATHY E	Shhhh!
HEATHCLIFF	Cathy!
CATHY E	Let's cross the moors and go to the Grange!
HEATHCLIFF	Where are you?
CATHY E	I'll race you!
HEATHCLIFF	I know you're here!
CATHY E	Hold me and we'll dance!
HEATHCLIFF	Cathy!
CATHY E	Just hold me!
HEATHCLIFF	Cathy!
CATHY E	Let me come home! Please let me come home!

(*Music fades. All* ACTORS *move, strike umbrellas and shawl and create a tableau around the window frame.*)

ACTOR 5	The day Catherine was buried made the last of the fine days for a month.
HEATHCLIFF	Cathy!
ACTOR 3	In the evening the weather broke; the wind shifted from south to north-east, bringing rain first, then sleet, and snow.
HEATHCLIFF	Cathy!

ACTOR 5	Inside Wuthering Heights. Isabella sat in a nook by the fire, quietly reading.
ACTOR 3	Whilst Hindley, lost in thought, stood across from her!
ACTOR 1	Cathy!
ACTOR 4	Heathcliff had been out on the moor and was desperate to enter the Heights . . .

(ACTOR 1 *takes up a position standing on the window seat behind the window, hands up as if attempting to push it open.*)

HEATHCLIFF	Let me in . . .
ISABELLA	He's back.
HINDLEY	(*a beat*) I'll keep him out five minutes, you won't object will you?
ISABELLA	You may keep him out the whole night for me.
HINDLEY	You and I have a great debt to settle with the man out yonder!
HEATHCLIFF	Isabella!
HINDLEY	Promise to hold your tongue and before the clock strikes you're a free woman.

(HINDLEY *takes out the pistol.*)

ISABELLA	You mustn't touch him. Let the door remain shut and be quiet.
HINDLEY	I've formed my resolution, and by God I'll execute it. Catherine is gone – nobody alive would regret me, or be ashamed – it's time to make an end.
HEATHCLIFF	Let me in!

(ISABELLA *shouts out to* HEATHCLIFF.)

ISABELLA   You'd better seek shelter somewhere else tonight.

HEATHCLIFF   Isabella!

ISABELLA   Mr Earnshaw has a mind to shoot you!

HEATHCLIFF   Open the door!

ISABELLA   Come in and get shot if you please! I've done my
                duty.

HINDLEY   You love him yet, you pathetic whore!

HEATHCLIFF   Isabella!

ISABELLA   I cannot commit murder, Mr Hindley stands
                sentinel!

HEATHCLIFF   Let me in by the kitchen!

ISABELLA   That's a poor love of yours that cannot bear a
                shower. If I were you I'd go and stretch myself over
                her grave and die like a faithful dog!

                (HEATHCLIFF *makes a violent movement as if kicking
                in the window. He makes an "oomph" noise. It is
                as if the kick has made contact with* HINDLEY *and
                he is sent reeling across the floor, letting go of the
                pistol.* ISABELLA *also collapses onto the floor.
                Although making no actual physical contact,*
                HEATHCLIFF *holds down* HINDLEY *with one hand.*)

HEATHCLIFF   Damn the both of you! You conspire with him
                against me, do you?

HINDLEY   Oh, if God would give me strength to strangle him in
                my last agony, I'd go to Hell with joy.

ISABELLA   It's enough that he has murdered one of you. Your
                sister would have been living now had it not been
                for him.

HEATHCLIFF   Get up!

ISABELLA   When I recollect how happy we were – how happy Catherine was before he came . . .

HEATHCLIFF   Get up, and be gone out of my sight!

ISABELLA   I loved Catherine too, and her brother requires attendance which for her sake I shall supply.

HEATHCLIFF   Get up, you wretched idiot, before I stamp you to death.

ISABELLA   Catherine could never have married you, never!

HEATHCLIFF   One more word and I'll kill you!

ISABELLA   What life would she have?

HEATHCLIFF   I'll kill you!

(HEATHCLIFF *lurches for* ISABELLA, *his hand raised.*)

HINDLEY   Leave her!

CATHY E   (*from where she is sitting*) Run! Isabella!

HEATHCLIFF   (*tormented, as if he can hear her*) Cathy!

CATHY E   Run . . . you never did belong here!

HEATHCLIFF   Cathy . . .

CATHY E   . . . Cross the moors and go to the Grange!

HEATHCLIFF   No . . . Cathy, please!

(*Lights.* ACTOR 1 *goes to sit.* ACTOR 3 *goes to sit.*)

ACTOR 5   In making her escape, Isabella flew down the steep road from Wuthering Heights . . .

ACTOR 3   . . . and across the moors towards the lights of the Grange.

(ACTOR 4 *moves downstage with a book and presents* ACTOR 5 *with a carpetbag.*)

ACTOR 4   When she entered, out of breath and crying, Edgar Linton was reading.

ISABELLA   Have the goodness to order the carriage to take me on to Gimmerton.

EDGAR   Isabella?

ISABELLA   I need to get away.

EDGAR   You can stay here.

ISABELLA   I daren't, he'll come and seek me and torment you. Besides, you wouldn't even write!

EDGAR   I know . . . I . . .

ISABELLA   Would you?

EDGAR   You must come and see our baby, please! Please do!

ISABELLA   No! You mustn't think I care little for Catherine – I've cried bitterly. We parted unreconciled and I shan't forgive myself. But I'm not going to feel sorry for Heathcliff.

HEATHCLIFF   (*desperate*) Cathy!

ISABELLA   I can't stay here, he couldn't bear to see me happy.

HEATHCLIFF   Oh, my love . . .

ISABELLA   I gave him my heart and he took it, pinched it to death and flung it back! And yet, he has wept tears of blood for Catherine. Promise you'll write . . . I need some clothes, a bonnet and a shawl! Go to the yard and have them prepare the carriage.

    (*Exit* ISABELLA *to sit.*)

EDGAR   Isabella, wait! Isabella!

(*Lights.*)

ISABELLA	Isabella's new abode was in the south, near London, (*A murmur of cockney chatter from other actors – "cor blimey", etc.*) where she had a son, born a few months subsequent to her escape.
ACTOR 2	He was christened Linton and was an ailing, peevish creature from the start!
ACTOR 3	Heathcliff discovered through servants Isabella's place of residence and the existence of his son.
ACTOR 4	But they wished for him to know nothing about the child!
ACTOR 3	Six months after his sister, Hindley Earnshaw died, (ACTORS 3 *and* 1 *put up umbrellas.*) drunk as a lord.
ACTOR 4	Barely twenty-seven . . .
ACTOR 5	. . . and in huge debt to Heathcliff!
ACTOR 2	His son, Hareton, was left penniless and fatherless.
ACTOR 3	And he lived, as a servant, at Wuthering Heights; deprived of wages and ignorant that he had ever been wronged.
ACTOR 2	Catherine Linton, on the other hand, was the most winning thing that ever brought sunshine into a desolate house.
ACTOR 5	Edgar Linton trusted her to no one!
ACTOR 4	Took her education on entirely himself and, until the age of thirteen, she had not once been out of the park that belonged to the Grange.

(ACTORS 3 *and* 1 *put down umbrellas and go to sit.* ACTOR 4 *goes to sit.* ACTORS 5 *and* 2 *assume roles of a now older* NELLY *and young* CATHY LINTON.)

CATHY L	How long will it be before I can walk to the top of those hills, Nelly? I wonder what lies on the other side – is it the sea?
NELLY	No, it's hills again! Just like these!
CATHY L	And what are those golden rocks like when you stand under them?
NELLY	That's Penistone Craggs. You couldn't climb them, they are too high!
CATHY L	I shall go on them when I'm older!
NELLY	They're not worth the trouble of visiting. The moors where you ramble with your papa are much nicer and Thrushcross Park is the nicest place in the world.
CATHY L	But I know the park and I don't know those.
NELLY	You'd be better staying here, miss . . .
CATHY L	Well, couldn't I go and look one day?
HEATHCLIFF	Maybe one day!

(EDGAR *enters the scene.*)

EDGAR	Cathy, I'm afraid Aunt Isabella is gravely ill!
CATHY L	Papa!
EDGAR	I must go to her at once!
CATHY L	But will you leave me here alone?
EDGAR	You'll have Nelly to keep you company.

(ACTOR 4 *sits.*)

CATHY L	Nelly, today I'm going to pretend to be an Arabian merchant crossing the desert with my caravan. I need you to give me plenty of provision for myself

and the camels and horses. That's what they have in the desert, I've read it in my books.

NELLY And keep your head covered, the desert can be hot and don't go beyond the park walls!

CATHY L How can I? The gate's locked.

NELLY Don't be late, either.

CATHY L I shall be back in time for tea!

(ACTOR 5 *goes to sit.*)

ACTOR 4 At tea, however, she never made an appearance.

ACTOR 2 She had leapt her pony over the lowest part of the hedge and galloped out of sight towards the Craggs.

(ACTOR 2 *sits on window seat as if on a horse. Other* ACTORS *make the sound of the horse rearing –* *"whoah!", etc.* ACTOR 2 *falls forward on to the floor as if being thrown from the horse.*)

ACTOR 3 It was further than she imagined and stumbling amongst the rocks she became lost and tired.

ACTOR 1 But she was rescued by a stranger: Hareton Earnshaw, now a lad of eighteen. He took her to recover . . .

ACTOR 4 . . . at Wuthering Heights!

(*Lights.* ACTOR 2 *remains on the floor.* ACTOR 3 *approaches as* HARETON.)

CATHY L It was further than I thought. I can see them from the Grange but I didn't imagine they'd be that far.

HARETON Aye, it's a good climb.

CATHY L It's a good job you found me; I think that I was quite lost.

HARETON	Have a rest, then I'll tek you back across moor.
ACTOR 4	Nelly had grown frantic with fear at Catherine's disappearance!
ACTOR 1	She struggled across the Heights to find Catherine.
	(ACTOR 5 *speaks to* CATHY *through the window frame.*)
NELLY	This is your last ride till papa comes back. I'll not trust you over the threshold again.
CATHY L	I don't care for I shall have a pretty story to tell tonight.
NELLY	The master's not at home then?
HARETON	No!
CATHY L	Have you been here before?
NELLY	You must come home at once!
CATHY L	What have I done?
NELLY	Let's have no petulance. You'll be left if you don't be quick, so please yourself. Where's your pony?
CATHY L	In the yard.
NELLY	Well, if you were aware whose house this is, you'd be glad enough to get out.
CATHY L	It's your father's, isn't it?
HARETON	No.
CATHY L	But you talked about our house and our folk. I thought you were the owner's son. You should have said if you're a servant. (*To* HARETON.) You'd better get my horse.
	(HARETON *does nothing.*)

What's the matter? Get my horse I say.

HARETON   I'll see thee damned before I be thy servant.

                 (*An intake of breath from* ACTORS 1 *and* 4.)

CATHY L   You'll see me what?

HARETON   Damned.

NELLY   There, you see, you've got into pretty company.
                 Nice words to be used to a young lady!

CATHY L   How dare you speak so to me. You wicked creature.
                 I shall tell papa what you said – now, bring the
                 pony!

NELLY   Softly, miss. You'll lose nothing by being civil. Mr
                 Hareton there is not the master's son . . . he's your
                 cousin.

CATHY L   My cousin?

NELLY   Yes.

CATHY L   Don't say such things. Papa has gone to fetch my
                 cousin from London. My cousin is a gentleman's
                 son.

NELLY   People can have many cousins of all sorts.

CATHY L   He's not my cousin. Look at him, how can he be?
                 I'll ask papa.

NELLY   No. He'll blame me for letting you come. Please, for
                 my sake, say nothing of this, believe me it's for the
                 best.

ACTOR 2   Cathy did keep the visit secret. It was not the right
                 time to tell her father.

ACTOR 4   For sooner than expected Isabella died.

                 (ACTORS 4 *and* 1 *put up umbrellas and stand.*)

ACTOR 3	Her last wish was that her brother take care of her son: Linton.
ACTOR 1	She was adamant she didn't want Heathcliff to have him.
ACTOR 4	And a day later, Edgar and a pale young Linton . . .
ACTOR 3	. . . arrived back at Thrushcross Grange.
	(ACTORS 4 *and* 1 *put down the umbrellas, shake them and sit.*)
CATHY L	Where's my cousin?
NELLY	He's tired, he's gone to bed.
CATHY L	Gone to bed, already? It's still daytime!
NELLY	It's been a long journey, your father is resting too.
CATHY L	Can I go and see them?
NELLY	Yes, but don't wake him, he's not so strong or merry as you are. Let him be quiet this evening at least.
CATHY L	But I've so much to ask him.
NELLY	Catherine . . .
CATHY L	Very well then, I'll just go see papa.
NELLY	Quietly!
	(*Exit* CATHY, *to sit.* ACTOR 4 *steps forward as* JOSEPH. *He coughs.*)
NELLY	Who's there?
JOSEPH	It was Joseph, Heathcliff's servant from the Heights! I need to speak to Mr Linton.
NELLY	God save us, you frightened me nearly to . . .

JOSEPH	Is he in?
NELLY	What do you want him for?
JOSEPH	Mr Heathcliff has sent me for his lad.
NELLY	What?
JOSEPH	His son Linton! And ah munt go back without him.
NELLY	His mother wanted him to come here, his health is very poor.
JOSEPH	Heathcliff's not bothered abaht his mother, he wants his lad and I mun tek him.
NELLY	Mr Linton is resting.
JOSEPH	Well, tell him if I don't tek him that tomorrow master'll come for him hissen. And he wunt want that would he? (*He laughs.*)
	(*Lights.* ACTOR 4 *goes to sit on window seat. He has become young* LINTON. ACTOR 5 *sits next to him as if on horse and carriage.* ACTOR 3 *stands behind them as if driving horses. It is a rough journey and they shout above the wind.*)
ACTOR 1	To avoid the danger of this threat being fulfilled, Edgar agreed that the boy be sent to his father the next morning.
ACTOR 3	Whoah! Nelly rode with him across the moor and did her best to keep his spirits up as they entered Wuthering Heights.
ACTOR 4	Linton was unaccustomed to the austerity of the Heights. (*Then, as* LINTON.) Mama never told me I had a father. I'd have rather have stayed with uncle. How am I to love papa? I don't know him.
NELLY	Well you must try and then he'll love you.
LINTON	Strange that he never came to see us.

(*"Whoah" as carriage reaches destination.* ACTORS
4 *and* 5 *are thrown forward out of the "carriage" to
standing positions.* ACTOR 3 *goes to sit. Lights.*
HEATHCLIFF *approaches.*)

HEATHCLIFF   God! What a beauty! What have they reared it on?
              Snails and sour milk? It's worse than I expected.
              Where's my share in you? Do you know me?

LINTON   No.

HEATHCLIFF   You've heard of me, I dare say?

LINTON   No.

HEATHCLIFF   Your mother was a wicked slut to leave you in
              ignorance of the sort of father you possessed.

NELLY   I hope you'll be kind to the boy, Mr Heathcliff.

HEATHCLIFF   You needn't fear. You're mine, and I want the
              triumph of seeing you lord of their estates.

LINTON   Don't leave me, please!

NELLY   Give him boiled milk or tea.

LINTON   I'll not stay here.

NELLY   And a little bread . . .

              (ACTOR 5 *goes to sit.*)

LINTON   Don't leave me! I'll not stay here!

              (ACTOR 3 *makes noise of wind.* ACTOR 2 *speaks as if
              ghost of* CATHERINE EARNSHAW.)

ACTOR 2   The night is darkening round you
              The wild winds coldly blow
              But a tyrant spell has bound you
              And you cannot, cannot go.

LINTON   . . . in this dark house!

ACTOR 2	The giant trees are bending Their bare boughs weighed with snow And the storm is fast descending And yet you cannot go.
HEATHCLIFF	Cathy . . .
ACTOR 2	Let me in, hold me and we will dance . . .
HEATHCLIFF	Cathy . . .
ACTOR 2	Just hold me!
LINTON	I can't stay here!

(LINTON *is weeping. Lights.*)

ACTOR 3	Edgar didn't tell Cathy the truth about her cousin Linton, despite her passionate tears.

(ACTOR 3 *gives* ACTOR 4 *a book, then goes to sit.*)

ACTOR 4	She was told only that he had gone to be with his father and, in time, his features waxed so dim in her memory that she would not have recognised him should she see him again.
ACTOR 1	And there was never rejoicing on the anniversary of her birth because it was also the anniversary of her mother's death.

(ACTOR 1 *goes to sit.*)

ACTOR 4	Invariably, Edgar spent that day sat alone in the library . . .

(ACTOR 4 *goes to sit.*)

ACTOR 5	. . . whilst Cathy and Nelly went up on to the moors.
ACTOR 2	Catherine was sixteen now and it was a beautiful spring day.

(*Lights.* CATHY *and* NELLY *are out of breath; they
have been climbing up the moors.*)

Somewhere near here there's a colony of moorhen.
I want to see whether they have made their nest.

NELLY   You're going too far, Miss Cathy, we must retrace
our steps!

CATHY L   Climb that hillock, pass that bank and by the time
you reach the other side I shall have raised the
birds. I think they're probably in the heather over
there near the Heights . . .

(CATHY *moves away from* NELLY. HEATHCLIFF *and*
HARETON *approach.* CATHY *backs into* HEATHCLIFF.
There is an "ooph" from ACTOR 4.)

HEATHCLIFF Plundering my grouse, are you?

CATHY L   No. I've neither taken any nor found any. Papa told
me they were up here and I wished to see the eggs.

HEATHCLIFF And who is your papa?

CATHY L   Mr Linton of Thrushcross Grange. I thought you
did not know me or you wouldn't have spoken in
that way.

HEATHCLIFF You suppose your papa is highly esteemed and
respected, then?

CATHY L   And what are you? That man I've seen before – is
he your son?

NELLY   Miss Cathy, we really must go back . . . !

HEATHCLIFF No. But I have a son and you've seen him before,
too. Will you walk to my house?

NELLY   . . . Miss . . .

CATHY L   He says I have seen his son . . .

NELLY	We should go back!
CATHY L	But he's mistaken, I think.
HEATHCLIFF	It will be a treat for her to look in on us.
NELLY	We really shouldn't!
HEATHCLIFF	Hareton, show her the way.
NELLY	Miss Cathy . . . !
HARETON	The path's well worn – it's over here!
CATHY L	Come Nelly, we won't be long.
	(ACTOR 4 *makes noise of wind.* CATHY *and* HARETON *move off to sit and also make noise of wind.*)
NELLY	(*having to speak above the wind*) You know you mean no good!
HEATHCLIFF	I want her to see Linton. We'll soon persuade her to keep the visit a secret, so where is the harm in it?
NELLY	The harm is her father would hate me if I had allowed her to enter your house.
HEATHCLIFF	I'm acting generously; the two cousins may meet, fall in love and get married, then she'll be very well provided for.
NELLY	But if Linton died, Catherine would be the heir . . .
HEATHCLIFF	No! His property would go to me.
NELLY	Why, then?
HEATHCLIFF	He took what was mine and now I shall take what is his!
ACTOR 4	(*still speaking as if above wind*) As they reached the Heights, Heathcliff hastened to open the door.

Linton stood on the hearth, his movements very
languid and his form extremely slight.

HEATHCLIFF   Now, who is that?

               (*Lights. Wind out.*)

CATHY L   Your son?

HEATHCLIFF   You've a short memory. Linton, don't you remember
               your cousin that you used to tease us so, with
               wishing to see?

CATHY L   Are you Linton?

LINTON   Yes, I am.

CATHY L   So you must be my uncle. You've been so near all
               this time. Why didn't you ever visit the Grange?

HEATHCLIFF   I visited it once or twice too often before you were
               born.

CATHY L   Well, I'll take this walk every morning in future – if I
               may? And sometimes I'll bring papa!

HEATHCLIFF   Mr Linton has a prejudice against me. We
               quarrelled at one time and if you tell him that you're
               coming here, he'll stop you. Therefore you must not
               mention it.

NELLY   I think we should go now!

CATHY L   Why did you quarrel?

HEATHCLIFF   He thought me too poor to wed his sister.

CATHY L   Well, I'll not come here then, Linton shall come to
               the Grange.

LINTON   It will be too far for me; to walk four miles would kill
               me.

CATHY L   Can you not ride?

HARETON   He can't do owt!

LINTON   You should come here, Miss Catherine.

HEATHCLIFF   Hareton, have you nothing to show your cousin?
Take her to see the dogs.

LINTON   Wouldn't you rather not sit?

HEATHCLIFF   Is he not a handsome lad? Go with her round the
farm. And behave like a gentleman! When you
speak say your words slowly and keep your hands
out of your pockets.

CATHY L   I'd like to see the horses first. Can I?

HARETON   Ar, if you must.

(CATHY *and* HARETON *move back slowly to form a*
tableau behind the window frame. They look up as
if reading an inscription above it.)

HEATHCLIFF   (*referring to* HARETON) I've a pleasure in him. He has
satisfied my expectations. He's no fool and I can
sympathise with all his feelings, having felt them
myself. Don't you think Hindley would be proud of
his son if he could see him?

NELLY   He'd be furious.

HEATHCLIFF   Almost as proud as I am of mine – but there's one
difference; one is gold put to the use of paving
stones and the other is tin, polished to ape a service
of silver. And the best is Hareton likes me – I've
out-matched Hindley there. (*To* LINTON.) Get up, you
idle boy. Go after the others and show Miss Cathy
your horse.

(ACTOR 4 *rises.* ACTOR 1 *goes to sit.*)

ACTOR 5   Outside in the yard Cathy inquired of Hareton,
what the inscription was over the door of Wuthering
Heights?

(ACTOR 5 *goes to sit.*)

HARETON   I don't know, I can't read it.

CATHY L   Can't read it? . . . It's English, but I want to know
                 why it's there.

                 (LINTON *giggles at* HARETON.)

LINTON   He doesn't know his letters. Can you believe in the
                 existence of such a dunce?

CATHY L   Is he all he should be? I think he doesn't understand
                 me. I can hardly understand him.

LINTON   There's nothing the matter but laziness, is there,
                 Earnshaw? My cousin fancies you are an idiot . . .
                 There you experience the consequence of scorning
                 "book-larning," as you would say . . . Have you
                 noticed his frightful Yorkshire pronunciation?

HARETON   Damn you!

                 (ACTORS 1 *and* 5 *react with an "ooh."*)

LINTON   Papa told you not to say bad words and you can't
                 open your mouth without one.

HARETON   If thou weren't more a lass than a lad, I'd fell thee
                 this minute.

                 (ACTOR 3 *goes to sit. Music. During the next lines*
                 ACTOR 1 *presents* ACTOR 4 *with a choice of books.*
                 He chooses one as if taking it from a shelf.)

ACTOR 1   Intrigued by her new found family, it was impossible
                 to tear Cathy away.

ACTOR 5   But despite Heathcliff's warnings to keep it a secret,
                 she wanted to know the truth from her father!

                 (*Lights.*)

CATHY L	Why was it that you didn't want me to go to Wuthering Heights? Was it because you disliked Mr Heathcliff?
EDGAR	No, it was not because I disliked Mr Heathcliff, but because Mr Heathcliff dislikes me and is the most diabolical man, delighting to wrong and ruin those he hates if they give him the slightest opportunity.
CATHY L	But I was always hoping that Linton was coming back.
EDGAR	You couldn't have seen him without being brought into contact with his father and I knew he would detest you on my account, so for your own good I made sure that you didn't see him again.
CATHY L	But Mr Heathcliff was quite cordial.
EDGAR	You think so?
CATHY L	He said I might come to his house when I pleased, only I mustn't tell you. You are the one to be blamed, father – he is willing for us to be friends, at least Linton and I – and you are not!
EDGAR	You will know hereafter why I wish you to avoid his house and family. Now think no more about them!
CATHY L	But . . .
EDGAR	No more!
	(He exits to sit.)
CATHY L	Nelly!
NELLY	What ever is it?
CATHY L	Papa. He says I'm not to go back to Wuthering Heights.
NELLY	It's not the end of the world.

CATHY L	But Linton expected to see me again and he'll be so disappointed. He'll wait for me and I shan't come.
NELLY	You've only seen him twice. He'll trouble himself no further about you.
CATHY L	I'll write a note to explain.
NELLY	Then he'd write you back and there'd never be an end of it.
CATHY L	The milk-fetcher can take it!
NELLY	It'll come to no good.
	(ACTOR 5 *freezes with her back to us at window seat.*)
ACTOR 3	Within days Cathy had received a mass of correspondence from Linton. She hid it away.
	(ACTOR 5 *comes out of freeze and confronts* CATHY *with some letters that she has taken from inside the window seat.*)
NELLY	A fine bundle of trash this is!
CATHY L	You've been through my things . . . how dare you!
NELLY	What do you suppose your father will think?
CATHY L	Don't show him.
NELLY	You must have led the way in writing such absurdities.
CATHY L	No, I didn't!
NELLY	Look at all this!
CATHY L	I didn't once think of loving him till . . .
NELLY	Loving him? You don't know him.

CATHY L	I do.
NELLY	You might as well talk of loving the miller who comes once a year to buy the corn.
CATHY L	Very well then, burn them.
NELLY	Now you're showing some sense.
CATHY L	But perhaps keep just one or two . . . for Linton's sake.
NELLY	No.
CATHY L	Nelly!
NELLY	No!
CATHY L	(*attempting to snatch one from her*) Just one!
NELLY	One we can show to papa?

(ACTOR 5 *slowly passes the letters to* ACTOR 4, *who has become* LINTON.)

ACTOR 1	The next morning it was Nelly, not Cathy, who wrote for the last time to Linton.
LINTON	(*reading*) Master Heathcliff is requested to send no more notes to Miss Catherine as she will not receive them! Said Linton, "Why papa? What have I done?"

(*Lights.* ACTORS 1 *and* 4 *go to sit.*)

ACTOR 2	Summer came to an end and Cathy, frightened by her little romance, had been considerably sadder and duller since its abandonment.
ACTOR 3	Along with this, her father's health had deteriorated. She had his companionship less and less and looked for solace on the moors.

(ACTOR 3 *gives* ACTOR 5 *an umbrella which she puts up. Seated actors make wind noises.*)

NELLY	It's starting to rain, miss. We must hurry back.
CATHY L	I like the rain . . .
NELLY	Come on, we can hold hands and run like we used to.
CATHY L	Not today . . .
NELLY	Cathy . . . ?
CATHY L	What will I do when I'm by myself?
NELLY	By yourself?
CATHY L	When papa is dead.
NELLY	But the master is young, there are years and years to come yet.
CATHY L	He's not well though, is he? Look at Aunt Isabella – she was younger than papa when she died!
NELLY	Aunt Isabella hadn't as much to live for.
	(HEATHCLIFF *approaches*.)
HEATHCLIFF	Miss Linton!
CATHY L	Quickly, we must go . . .
HEATHCLIFF	Don't be in haste. I have something to ask you.
CATHY L	I shan't speak to you, Mr Heathcliff.
HEATHCLIFF	But I've got your letters and if you give me any pertness I'll send them to your dear papa.
NELLY	Miss Cathy, come!
HEATHCLIFF	You've broken Linton's heart with your fickleness. Unless you restore him, he'll die.

NELLY How can you lie so?

HEATHCLIFF I tell the truth.

NELLY It's impossible that a person should die for love of a stranger.

HEATHCLIFF How would you know?

NELLY Miss Cathy!

HEATHCLIFF I shall be from home all this week. Go and see if I have not spoken the truth.

NELLY Don't listen. Now hurry or we'll be soaked.

(*Wind noises die out through speech.*)

ACTOR 2 The rainy night ushered in a misty morning. Cathy had not slept for thinking of her poor cousin. At dawn she crept from the house and, driven by guilt, she made her way across the moor . . .

ACTOR 4 . . . to Wuthering Heights!

(*Lights.* ACTOR 3 *has become* HARETON.)

HARETON You want?

CATHY L Linton!

HARETON Hey, I can read, nah! That inscription about the door, I know what it says, nah!

CATHY L You are grown clever then!

HARETON It says my name, Hareton Earnshaw.

CATHY L And what about the numbers above it?

HARETON Be reight, I don't know mi numbers yet.

CATHY L So you are still the dunce . . . ?

HARETON   I'll get Linton you! (*Shouts.*) Linton . . . somebody
                 to see you . . . Linton!

                 (HARETON *exits to sit and* ACTOR 4 *enters slowly as*
                 LINTON.)

LINTON   You've come. Father said that you would.

CATHY L   How are you?

                 (*She moves to embrace him.*)

LINTON   Don't kiss me.

CATHY L   Aren't you glad to see me?

LINTON   You should have come instead of writing.

CATHY L   I couldn't . . .

LINTON   You don't despise me, do you?

CATHY L   No. Next to Papa I love you better than anybody
                 living. But I daren't come when Mr Heathcliff
                 returns. Will he stay away many days?

LINTON   No. But he frequently goes on the moors.

CATHY L   I wish you were my brother.

LINTON   I'd rather you were my wife.

CATHY L   Your wife? People hate their wives sometimes! Mr
                 Heathcliff must have been wicked to Aunt Isabella
                 to make her leave him as she did.

LINTON   She didn't leave him.

CATHY L   Of course she did!

LINTON   Don't say that!

CATHY L   But it's the truth.

LINTON	Well, I'll tell you something! Your mother hated your father!
CATHY L	Don't be silly.
LINTON	And loved mine!
CATHY L	That's absurd. Why are you saying this?
LINTON	Because that's the truth.
CATHY L	You little liar!
LINTON	She did!
CATHY L	That's your father's tale too, I suppose.
LINTON	She did, she did!

(CATHY *slaps him. Again it is stylised.* LINTON *collapses onto the window seat, coughing.*)

You've hurt me. Even Hareton never touches me. He never struck me in his life.

CATHY L	I didn't strike you. And you couldn't have been hurt by that.
LINTON	I can't speak to you. (*He coughs again.*)
CATHY L	You shouldn't have said what you did! Do you want me to go?
LINTON	We'll speak no more of it.
CATHY L	Yes, that would be for the best. Would you like me to read to you for a while?

(HARETON *enters.*)

HARETON	If you're reading, go to your room! I want to sit in here.
LINTON	It's my house, why should I? We'll do as we like.

HARETON	I said to tek her to your room!
CATHY L	Come on, Linton. Ignore him.
LINTON	(*trembling*) No. Let us stay or I'll kill you!
HARETON	I'd like to see that.
LINTON	I will. I'll kill you. I will!

(HARETON *makes a quick, threatening move towards* LINTON, *which makes him jump and sets him off coughing again.*)

HARETON	You'd better go home.
CATHY L	What have you done?
HARETON	He'll be reight.
CATHY L	Oh, Linton. (*To* HARETON.) I'll tell papa, then you'll be put in prison and hanged.
HARETON	(*upset*) Miss Catherine . . . please . . .

(*He exits to sit.*)

CATHY L	You will!

(LINTON *is coming round. He is coughing again.*)

Oh, Linton . . .

LINTON	Leave me.
CATHY L	Shall I get you some water?
LINTON	No . . . you have caused too much trouble already. Just being here. You torment Hareton.
CATHY L	Then I'll go. Tell your father that you have no wish to see me any more.
LINTON	No!

CATHY L	Then what? What do you want? I don't understand.
	(*Pause.*)
LINTON	I feel so cross and bitter. I say things that I don't mean. Believe me, if I might be as kind and as good as you are I would be, more so than healthy. But it's hard, it's in my nature. I'm sorry. I love you and will do till I die.
	(*He takes* CATHY'S *hand. They freeze.*)
ACTOR 5	By the end of the summer Edgar's health had worsened and he had discovered Catherine's secret.
ACTOR 1	But realising he was unable to stop her, he agreed that she could continue to meet her cousin, but only midway, on land that belonged to the Grange.
ACTOR 4	Linton, however, unable to travel far, soon broke these rules and Catherine found herself meeting him at Wuthering Heights whenever she thought Heathcliff was out!
	(ACTORS 2 *and* 4 *sit, laughing.* HEATHCLIFF *has approached.*)
HEATHCLIFF	Get up! Get up, don't grovel on the ground.
LINTON	I can't.
HEATHCLIFF	Damn you! Get up!
LINTON	I will, only let me alone. I've done as you wished. Catherine will tell you that I have been cheerful. Keep by me, Catherine. Give me your hand.
HEATHCLIFF	Take mine. You would imagine that I was the Devil himself, Miss Linton. He shudders at my touch. You shall have some tea, Miss Linton!
CATHY L	No, thank you.
HEATHCLIFF	But I'd like some company.

CATHY L	No.

| HEATHCLIFF | The door is locked! |

| CATHY L | I'm not afraid of you. And I wouldn't eat or drink here if I were starving. Now Linton's resting, let me go. |

(She attempts to get past him.)

| HEATHCLIFF | Stand back or I shall knock you down. |

| CATHY L | Let me go! |

(They struggle again. She bites him, and he slaps her a number of times. Again, this is from a distance but her body reacts to the slap each time and she falls to the ground.)

| LINTON | Father! |

| HEATHCLIFF | Stay here with Linton. I'll give you what I have. I shall be your father tomorrow – all the father you have in a few days! |

| CATHY L | No. |

| HEATHCLIFF | Think carefully. (*A beat.*) I'm going out to seek your horse. |

(HEATHCLIFF *exits.*)

| CATHY L | (*through tears*) You must tell me what your father wants. It was for your sake I came. |

| LINTON | He wants us to be married, and he's afraid of me dying if we wait. |

| CATHY L | Married! |

| LINTON | You are to stay here, and if you do as he wishes, you shall return home and take me with you. |

| CATHY L | What? |

LINTON	Won't you save me – let me come to the Grange? You must obey my father!
CATHY L	I must obey my own. He'll be worried if I don't return; he'll be distressed already. And I love papa better than you.

(*Re-enter* HEATHCLIFF.)

HEATHCLIFF	I'm afraid your beast looks like it's trotted off. There was a servant sent to seek you from the Grange, but you've missed him. You should have opened a lattice and called out. Now, Linton! Snivelling again? Go to your room.

(LINTON *goes to sit.*)

HEATHCLIFF	(*to* CATHY) Are you still not afraid of me?
CATHY L	Mr Heathcliff, let me go home! I promise to marry Linton – papa would like me to, and I love him – and why should you wish to force what I would willingly do myself?
HEATHCLIFF	I shall enjoy myself in thinking your father will be miserable. You could have hit on no surer way of fixing your residence here.
CATHY L	Then send someone to let him know I'm safe. Or let us marry now. If he died before I returned I couldn't bear to live. I'm going to kneel here at your feet and I'll not get up, or take my eyes from your face till you look at me! Don't turn away! Look! I don't hate you, I'm not angry that you struck me. Have you never loved anybody in your life? Never?
HEATHCLIFF	How little you know!
CATHY L	Look at me, just once, and show me some pity!
HEATHCLIFF	I detest you!

(*For a moment he sees her mother in her face and goes to touch it, but then catches himself.*)

I cursed you for coming into the world! When your father dies Linton shall be master of the Grange and everything you have shall be his!

CATHY L Mr Heathcliff!

(CATHY *cries, but her tears become false laughter as she forms a wedding tableau with* ACTORS 5 *and* 4 *within the frame of the window.* ACTOR 5 *gives* ACTOR 2 *a posy of flowers.* ACTOR 3 *becomes a Victorian photographer.*)

ACTOR 3 And . . .

(*He takes the photograph.*)

Cathy remained a prisoner for five nights after the wedding until a message was sent to the Grange.

ACTOR 1 It told how she had been found in the marsh and was recuperating – thanks to Mr Heathcliff – at Wuthering Heights.

(*Lights.* ACTOR 1 *puts up an umbrella and gives it to* ACTOR 4. *He then goes to sit.*)

ACTOR 4 Edgar sent Nelly to bring her home immediately. His illness had progressed and he'd been told by the doctor that he hadn't much longer to live.

(ACTOR 4 *walks slowly past* CATHY *to his seat, handing the umbrella to* ACTOR 5 *as he passes her.*)

CATHY L Papa . . . oh papa, I'm so sorry, I . . .

(*She throws down the flowers as if on a grave.* ACTORS 3 *and* 4 *make noise of the wind.* HEATHCLIFF *approaches.*)

HEATHCLIFF I'm come to fetch you home; and I hope you'll be a dutiful daughter.

NELLY Why not let Catherine continue here and send Master Linton to her?

HEATHCLIFF   I'm seeking a tenant for the Grange – besides, I want my children about me. Make haste and get ready to go.

CATHY L   I shall be happy to. Linton is all I have left to love in the world, and you shan't make me hate him.

HEATHCLIFF   He'll do that himself.

CATHY L   I know he has bad nature, he's your son. But he doesn't love you. Nobody does. You are miserable and lonely. Nobody will cry for you when you die!

HEATHCLIFF   Get your things.

               (*Exit* CATHY, *to sit.*)

NELLY   Let me come with her.

HEATHCLIFF   She doesn't need you. She needs me to put her in her place!

NELLY   And is that what her mother would have wanted?

HEATHCLIFF   If it wasn't for her, her mother would still be alive!

NELLY   Don't say such things!

HEATHCLIFF   Do you know what I did yesterday? I got the sexton who was digging Edgar Linton's grave to remove the earth off Cathy's coffin lid and I opened it. I thought once I would have stayed there when I saw her face again – it is hers yet – but had the air blown on it, it would have changed. So I struck one side of the coffin loose and covered it up – not Edgar's side, damn him! – and I bribed the sexton to pull it away, when I'm laid there, and slide mine out, too.

NELLY   Were you not ashamed to disturb the dead?

HEATHCLIFF   She has disturbed me, night and day through eighteen years – incessantly, remorselessly, killing me, driving me mad.

(ACTOR 2 *becomes the ghost of* CATHERINE EARNSHAW. *She is seen only by* HEATHCLIFF. *She appears in the frame of the window. He watches her. The wind stops.*)

ACTOR 2   I'll not pity you.

HEATHCLIFF   Hear!

ACTOR 2   I'll not pity you!

HEATHCLIFF   Hear! Do you hear her? Do you hear her ghost?

NELLY   No.

(ACTOR 2 *laughs and exits to sit.* ACTORS 4 *and* 3 *also laugh.* ACTOR 5 *puts down umbrella and goes to sit.*)

ACTOR 2   I'll not pity you!

(ACTOR 1 *crouches, head in hands.*)

ACTOR 3   When Cathy Linton arrived back at the Heights she ran upstairs and shut herself immediately in Linton's room.

ACTOR 4   He could barely breathe and never left his bed.

(ACTOR 4 *takes with him a closed umbrella and goes to sit on the upstage side of the window seat with his back to us. He leans against the frame.* ACTOR 2 *is with him.*)

ACTOR 5   Still in shock at the death of her father, she nursed Linton with great tenderness until she became frightened and pleaded for help.

(*Wind whistles from* ACTORS 3 *and* 5.)

CATHY L   Mr Heathcliff! Mr Heathcliff! Could the doctor be sent for? Linton is very ill.

HEATHCLIFF   There's nothing the doctor can do.

CATHY L	You don't know that.
HEATHCLIFF	Doctors cost money.
CATHY L	If nobody will help me, he'll die.
	(*A pause.* HEATHCLIFF *says nothing.*)
	He'll die. Soon, today, tonight! He is your son!
	(ACTOR 4 *rises and walks downstage away from* CATHY *and the window. He puts up the umbrella.*)
CATHY L	Don't you leave me, Linton – you can't, not here on my own. There's been so little time; why so soon? We could go on the moors. Why have you given in? Why? Please, Linton! Please . . .
HEATHCLIFF	Too late.
	(*A beat. The wind dies.*)
	How do you feel?
	(CATHY *is dumb.*)
	How do you feel, Catherine?
CATHY L	I feel and see only death!
	(ACTOR 4 *puts down the umbrella, then goes to sit. Lights.*)
ACTOR 3	Cathy stayed upstairs in the Heights for a fortnight.
ACTOR 4	And when Heathcliff showed her the Will, she discovered that all of Linton's property and what had been hers before their marriage went to him.
ACTOR 5	On the first occasion of her coming downstairs, Heathcliff had gone to the Grange . . . and Hareton was mending the floor.
	(ACTOR 3 *hammers at the floor.*)

CATHY L   I cannot bear any longer being in the cold.

HARETON   Sit by the fire, then.

           (CATHY *sits downstage centre on the floor.* ACTOR 3 *collects a book from* ACTOR 5.)

           Here, I got you this book.

           (CATHY *snatches it from him without thanking him.* HARETON *stands close, watching her. She turns the pages of the book. He is fascinated by her and eventually puts out his hand and strokes one of her curls, as gently as if it was a bird.*)

CATHY L   Get away! How dare you touch me! I'll go back upstairs again if you come near me.

           (HARETON, *embarrassed, recoils. Then . . .*)

HARETON   Will you read to me? I'd like to hear summat.

CATHY L   Don't pretend to be kind to me now. I would have given my life for one kind word, even to see your face, but you kept away. I'm driven down here by the cold, not either to amuse you or enjoy your company.

HARETON   What could I have done?

CATHY L   Oh, you are an exception, I never missed such a concern as you.

HARETON   I offered more than once, I asked Heathcliff . . .

CATHY L   Be silent! I'll go out of doors or anywhere, rather than have your voice in my head!

HARETON   (*mutters*) Go to Hell, then.

           (*He moves away upstage.*)

CATHY L   Running to tell your master of me, are you?

HARETON   He's never here.

                 (ACTOR 3 *goes to sit.* ACTOR 2 *freezes.*)

ACTOR 4   Heathcliff had become withdrawn and, more and
                 more, preferred his own company, disappearing for
                 hours onto the moors.

                 (*Lights.* HEATHCLIFF, *distraught and disturbed,
                 stands on the window seat. Other actors make the
                 noise of the wind.*)

HEATHCLIFF   I can feel a change approaching, Cathy. I'm in its
                 shadow at present – I take so little interest in
                 everyday life that I hardly remember to eat and drink.
                 Hareton and your daughter cause me such pain. I
                 wish she were invisible, and his startling
                 resemblance to you connects him so much to you.
                 But then what is not connected with you to me? I
                 cannot look down on the floor but your features are
                 shaped on the flags! In every cloud and every tree –
                 filling the air at night and caught by glimpses in
                 every object – I'm surrounded with your image.

ACTORS 2, 3, 4, 5 (*whispered*) You killed me. You broke my heart.

HEATHCLIFF   Don't blame me. Just stay with me.

ACTORS 2, 3, 4, 5 I can't . . .

HEATHCLIFF   Cathy! Cathy!

                 (*Wind out. Lights.* HARETON *approaches* CATHY *with
                 more books. He throws them down at her.*)

HARETON   Here! Have them! Seeing as you'll not talk, you
                 might as well have these. They're no use to me.

                 (HARETON *turns to exit.*)

CATHY L   Do you ever dream, Hareton?

HARETON   Eh?

CATHY L	And if you do, what is it about?
	(HARETON *looks at her but does not answer.*)
	Are you dreaming now?
HARETON	I want nowt to do wi' you!
CATHY L	Why do you need to be so cross to me?
HARETON	You can tek it or leave it.
CATHY L	When I call you stupid, I don't mean anything.
	(*He laughs.*)
	It's good to want to read.
HARETON	Go to Hell!
CATHY L	(*a pause*) We should be friends.
HARETON	Friends! You hate me and think I'm not fit enough to wipe your shoe!
CATHY L	It is not I who hate you, it is you who hate me!
HARETON	You're a liar! Why have I made Heathcliff angry by taking your part a hundred times?
CATHY L	I didn't know you took my part. I was miserable and bitter at everybody. (*A pause.*) Forgive me.
	(CATHY *extends her hand.* HARETON *does not move and keeps his eyes fixed firmly on the ground.* CATHY *remains an instant, undecided what to do, but then instinctively kisses him on the cheek.* HARETON *continues not to look up.* CATHY *takes a book and offers it to him.*)
	If you take this, I'll teach you to read.
	(*Very slowly,* HARETON *reaches for the book.*)

Say you'll forgive me. You'd make me happy.

(HARETON *mutters something inaudible, his face changed now, his harshness and rudeness gone.*)

And you'll be my friend?

HARETON   You'll be ashamed of me every day of your life.

CATHY L   So you won't be my friend?

(*They laugh.* HEATHCLIFF *has observed the end of this scene. They stop laughing and stare at* HEATHCLIFF.)

HEATHCLIFF   I thought I cured you of laughing.

CATHY L   I'm sorry . . . Mr Heathcliff!

HARETON   It was my fault.

HEATHCLIFF   Joseph needs some help in the barn, you!

(HEATHCLIFF *holds his hand out for* HARETON *to give him the book.* HARETON *gives him it and exits to stand behind the window frame.* HEATHCLIFF *repeats the same gesture to* CATHY. *She gives him her books and goes to stand in front of the window frame, allowing her eyes to meet* HARETON'S.)

ACTOR 1   As Heathcliff grew more and more disinclined to society, Cathy and Hareton became good friends.

(CATHY *and* HARETON *laugh.* HARETON *moves downstage as if doing the garden,* CATHY *watching and helping.* HEATHCLIFF *approaches.*)

HARETON   How's that looking?

CATHY L   Aren't you tired?

HARETON   No, I'm reight!

(HEATHCLIFF *enters. Silence.*)

HEATHCLIFF	Why have you touched the trees?
HARETON	I've pulled up two or three bushes, but I'm going to set 'em again.
HEATHCLIFF	Why have you pulled them up?
CATHY L	We wanted to plant some flowers. I'm the only person to blame. I wished him to do it.
HEATHCLIFF	And who gave you leave to make decisions?
CATHY L	Well . . .
HEATHCLIFF	And who ordered you to obey?
CATHY L	You shouldn't grudge me a few yard of earth when you have taken all my land!
HEATHCLIFF	Your land! You never had any land!
CATHY L	And my money.
HEATHCLIFF	Get done and begone!
CATHY L	If you strike me, he'll strike you!
HEATHCLIFF	How dare you pretend to rouse him against me. I'll kill you . . .
HARETON	(*whispers*) Don't . . .
CATHY L	He'll not obey you any more and he'll soon detest you as much as I do.
HARETON	Shhhh . . . have done.
	(*It is too late.* HEATHCLIFF *catches her by the hair.*)
HEATHCLIFF	This time you have provoked me when I cannot bear it.
HARETON	Don't . . .

(*There is a struggle, but suddenly* HEATHCLIFF *releases her, takes a moment to collect himself, then is calm.*)

HEATHCLIFF   You must learn to avoid putting me into a passion or I shall really murder you. As for Hareton – your love will make him an outcast and a beggar . . . Now begone!

(HARETON *and* CATHY *exit to sit.* ACTORS 2, 3 *and* 4 *start noise of wind.* ACTOR 5 *has entered as* NELLY *to see what the commotion is.*)

NELLY   Are you alright?

HEATHCLIFF   Yes.

NELLY   You have no feelings of illness, have you?

HEATHCLIFF   I wish I had, then I might die.

NELLY   Are you not afraid?

HEATHCLIFF   I have neither fear, nor hope of death – why should I? But with my constitution, I should remain above ground till there is scarcely a black hair on my head. And yet I cannot continue in this condition. I have to remind myself to breathe, to remind my heart to beat. I'm going mad.

(*Noise of wind from other* ACTORS *and whispers of* "*Heathcliff.*")

Cathy!

NELLY   Mr Heathcliff!

HEATHCLIFF   Catherine . . .

NELLY   Mr Heathcliff!

HEATHCLIFF   It's time, Nelly.

NELLY	Time for what? You'll be spared to repent of your many injustices yet!
HEATHCLIFF	It's not my fault that I cannot eat or rest. I'll do both as soon as I possibly can. I'm happy, but not yet happy enough.
NELLY	Strange happiness. Take advice on how you might be happier.
HEATHCLIFF	Give it.
NELLY	From thirteen years old, you have lived a selfish, unchristian life. Send for the minister, make a change . . .
HEATHCLIFF	I need only someone to know how I might be buried.
NELLY	Don't talk of such things.
HEATHCLIFF	Please. You need to know. Carry me to the churchyard in the evening. Let only Hareton and Joseph accompany me. Make sure that sexton obeys my directions concerning the two coffins, but no minister need come, nor anything be said over me. I have nearly attained my Heaven and that of others is altogether unvalued and uncoveted by me.

(Music – Haydn.)

ACTOR 5	That night, a storm was brewing and as the rain began beating on the lattice he could be heard to be crying out, as if in pain.

(ACTOR 2 appears at the window, as at the beginning.)

HEATHCLIFF	Cathy!
CATHY E	Let me in! Let me in! I lost my way on the moor! Open the window and let me in! Twenty years, it's been. I've been a waif for twenty years!
HEATHCLIFF	Cathy!

CATHY E   I've come home!

                   (HEATHCLIFF *walks slowly to* CATHY. *They embrace,
                   her still standing in the window, him below her.
                   She cradles his head.*)

ACTOR 5   (*whispered*) Heathcliff!

ACTOR 3   (*whispered*) Call the doctor!

ACTOR 4   (*whispered*) He'll not let us in!

ACTOR 5   (*whispered*) Heathcliff!

ACTOR 4   (*whispered*) The devil's carried off his soul!

                   (CATHY *and* HEATHCLIFF *freeze. Lights. Silence.*
                   ACTORS 3, 4 *and* 5 *slowly walk downstage and put
                   up umbrellas.*)

ACTOR 3   He was buried, to the scandal of the whole
                   neighbourhood, as he had wished. And there are
                   now three headstones on the slope next to the moor.

ACTOR 5   Cathy and Hareton married and moved to the
                   Grange. Only Heathcliff's old servant, Joseph,
                   would remain at Wuthering Heights. He would live
                   in the kitchen and the rest would be shut up.

ACTOR 2   For the use of such ghosts as choose to inhabit it.

ACTOR 1   You see, folks round here swear that Heathcliff
                   walks – him and a woman, they say.

ACTOR 4   But if you stand on the moors and listen to the soft
                   wind breathing through the grass – it is hard to ever
                   imagine unquiet slumbers for the sleepers in that
                   quiet earth.

ACTOR 5   Long or short though life may be
                   'Tis nothing to eternity.
                   We part blow to meet on high
                   Where blissful ages never die.

(ACTORS *make sound of wind. All* ACTORS *exit in the
same manner as they entered at the beginning,
struggling to put their umbrellas down and blown
by the wind.* ACTOR 3 *is left stage centre. He puts
down his umbrella. The wind stops. He looks at the
audience and smiles. Blackout.*)

THE END